SHARING OUR FAITH WITH *Without* FRIENDS *Losing Either*

OTHER TITLES IN THE
NAD CHURCH MINISTRIES SERIES

SHARING OUR FAITH WITH *Without* FRIENDS *Losing Either*

By
MONTE SAHLIN

Review and Herald® Publishing Association
Washington, DC 20039-0555
Hagerstown, MD 21740

The author assumes full responsibility for the accuracy of all facts
and quotations as cited in this book.

Texts credited to NIV are from the *Holy Bible, New International
Version.* Copyright © 1973, 1978, by the International Bible Society.
Used by permission of Zondervan Bible Publishers.

Edited by John R. Calkins
Designed by Bill Kirstein
Cover art by Denny Bond

PRINTED IN U.S.A.

95 94 93 92   •   10 9 8 7 6 5 4 3 2

R & H Cataloging Service
Sahlin, Monte
 Sharing our faith with friends without losing
either: what the fastest growing Adventist churches
know.

1. Personal evangelism. I. Title.
253.7

ISBN 0-8280-0600-8

Contents

Dedication

To those congregations, pastors, and church members who have so faithfully, cheerfully, and openly shared with me their lives and answered questions and questionnaires.

To Norma, Stephanie, and Melissa for sharing husband and father with the word processor.

Acknowledgments

To the editors of *Adventist Review, Ministry,* and *Celebration!* for publishing early versions of some of the research in this volume.

To Harold Lee, Philip Follett, and James Zackrison for their critical reading of the manuscript and helpful input.

Foreword

MAYOR RICHARD Daley, perhaps one of the most effective mayors in American history, often used to say, "All politics is local." We are coming to see in North America that all real church growth is local. It takes place in the local congregation where the people meet together in Christ's name. No program can be called successful unless it has results in and through the local congregation.

This has been the emphasis in North America for some time, and it must be even greater in the days ahead. As far back as 1979 when North American Division leadership scheduled a summit session on evangelism and church growth, we were saying that "the real action units of the church are the local churches. . . . It is the purpose of the General Conference/North American Division, the union conferences, and the local conferences to serve as . . . support centers in providing coordinated resource materials and personnel, and to provide training sessions collectively and individually as needed and arranged with the local church." We have included this concept in our statement of mission and strategy.

Now comes a new book by Monte Sahlin, adult ministries coordinator for North American Division Church Ministries, that brings it all together. The book reports the thought and work of many who are endeavoring to build a constantly more effective evangelistic strategy and includes pastors, lay leaders, and denominational staff.

The author brings to his task a rich experience in pastoral, evangelistic, and community service ministries. He has been involved in many of the experimental evangelistic projects in the North American Division over the past 20 years and has pastored inner city, suburban, and small town churches ranging in size from 17 to 500 members.

Sharing Our Faith With Friends Without Losing Either is much needed. These challenging times demand much more from pastors and church members than ever before. Just think of the challenges. Evangelism—opening the Scriptures to the people—is the most important work of all. We have also been saying that for many years. But what makes this book different is its unique relational approach to outreach ministries.

You will enjoy Sahlin's book. There is a wealth of information here. The focus is always on Christ's mission in the local congregation. And it is more than theory. There are reports of many exciting happenings in our church today. And it is, above all, practical. All kinds of doables. Strategies that have worked. If you want to find renewal and growth, and experience the thrill and excitement of a church that's going places, you need to get into the principles, the basics, that are enunciated in this volume.

Some Adventists complain that it is impossible to do effective evangelism in this secular society. But we mustn't overlook what the Holy Spirit is doing. I can recommend this book wholeheartedly. I keep thinking of all those spiritual gifts that God has placed in His church. Every one of us is endowed. I keep thinking also that a gift is a terrible thing to waste.

Years ago the pastor did everything. He was the preacher, teacher, counselor—pitcher, catcher, batter, coach, and umpire—and the church members watched. Unfortunately, the preacher ran himself out because he tried to take over the whole game. Now there is a new brand of preacher out there. He's challenging us. He's telling us, "You shouldn't be sitting and watching. You should be participating. In fact, you should be in the vanguard."

Charles E. Bradford, President
North American Division of the General Conference

INTRODUCTION

The Third Era of Adventist Evangelism

THE 1980s have been a watershed period in the evangelization of North America by Seventh-day Adventists. Beginning with the summit meeting on evangelism convened by the newly elected president of the North American Division, Charles E. Bradford, in April 1979 at Glacier View, Colorado, it has been a time of change, a slow transition between an old order featuring conventional ways of doing evangelism that have worked well for several decades and a new order that is not yet fully discerned.

With the publication of Dr. Gottfried Oosterwal's groundbreaking research in 1976—*Patterns of Seventh-day Adventist Church Growth in North America*—and the voting of a document entitled "Evangelism and Finishing God's Work" at the 1976 Annual Council, the stage was set for rethinking the evangelistic strategy of the church. "We must face honestly certain obstacles that stand in the way of a finished work," the document said. Among the 14 obstacles noted were: "expenditure of time, talent, money, and energies on maintenance rather than advance"; "failure to enable full participation in ministry by all the laity"; "the imbalance between those whose efforts are directed inward toward church members and those whose efforts are directed outward toward filling community needs and saving the lost"; "the misallocation of high priority resources to low productive activities";

"the insufficient number of congregations within geographic and cultural distance of the populations we are seeking to win"; "insufficient diagnosis and evaluation of existing programs"; and "lack of creative research and development." The document mandated changes in funding and personnel and asked that steps be taken to "clarify the role of the pastor," "enable laity to function as ministers," "multiply churches among receptive people," and "tailor ministries to particular homogeneous units."

At the summit meeting, which included all of the union and local conference presidents, each of these topics was given attention. Much time was spent in prayer for the guidance of the Holy Spirit, and Bible study focused on the nature and purpose of the church. Along with devotionals on the church as "people in community," the "place where the Spirit dwells," and "people in mission," Dr. Oosterwal presented four major papers on a theology of mission. The Bible's definition of the church and its mission, the church in creative tension with the world, the role of the laity and the growth of the church were discussed in these papers, parts of which have been published in *Ministry,* used in countless seminar syllabi, and formed the basis of a number of official pronouncements. Significant portions of the meeting were spent in small discussion groups in which the assembled presidents and a handful of resource staff struggled with these theological concepts and how to infuse them into the Adventist church.

No official document came from the summit, but a *Faith, Action, Advance* handbook was published about a year later, which reflects the consensus at the meeting. "The local church is the basic unit of organization and the focus of all activity [in the denomination]," it declared. "Church growth comes from recognition and development of spiritual gifts, through small groups, by the priorities of Word, worship, fellowship, and service." Much of the book dealt with the details of how denominational departments and programs might focus on supporting the local church in its growth. A more concise document was prepared by the NAD staff in 1981, entitled "The Church as One Organization." Unfortunately, it was never widely circulated.

One of the immediate outcomes of the evangelism strategy summit was the creation of the Institute of Church Ministry as part of the seminary at Andrews University. It became a permanent research facility that has generated more than three dozen studies of Adventist church growth in North America—a mountain of evidence about what works and what doesn't work. The sheer volume of the information has resulted in much of it remaining unfamiliar to the very practitioners and planners who need it.[1]

The first study, completed by the new institute in April 1981, will continue to be the benchmark for research into Adventist church growth in the decades ahead. It was the first church growth research project in any denomination, or by any interdenominational institution, to use such modern statistical tools as regression analysis. This tool identified the key factors and clusters of factors related to church growth in "average" congregations as well as "superchurches" with spectacular growth stories.

More than 8,000 church members returned questionnaires in this survey of 193 randomly selected local churches. The results indicate that the following factors are vital to growth in Adventist congregations in North America:

1. Intentionality. The pastor focuses on church growth. The church board establishes a plan for growth. The members want to grow, see their congregation as a soul-winning church, and sense that their pastor places high priority on outreach.

2. Small groups. Especially in White churches, the key activity related to church growth is participation by a significant portion of the congregation in small Bible study and fellowship groups.

3. Involvement. Growing congregations have a high percentage of members who hold church offices or are active in ministries sponsored by the church, especially in giving Bible studies and helping with midweek meetings and public seminars.

4. Fellowship. A surprising characteristic among growing churches is that the pastor spends less time in ministry to members and in church administration, yet a greater sense of unity exists among members, with a stronger feeling of assurance that they are right with God. Obviously a lot of pastoral care and leadership is being accomplished through the group process and the enabling of lay ministry, instead of traditional one-to-one pastoral activities.

5. Inclusiveness. New members abound in these congregations, and the established members feel good about it. In these churches, the pastor holds a variety of effective reaping meetings, skillfully getting decisions and carefully assimilating converts.

6. Demographics. Although Hispanic and Black congregations have higher growth rates than White ones, the Adventist Church is making some headway in reaching the middle class. Churches with higher growth rates tend to have more affluent members.

In the creative atmosphere of the summit meeting, Texas pastor Harry Robinson was encouraged by his president to experiment with a "seminar" approach in evangelism. These Revelation seminars resembled adult education classes or business seminars more than traditional crusades. Attendees were handed notebooks and sat at tables, classroom-style. With no song service or special music, time was allowed for questions, and sessions ended with a quiz. Robinson was careful to document trials of the new approach and provide formulas to predict the number of attendees per thousand mailers sent; how many would continue and the number of expected baptisms. These prepackaged materials and mailers produced by the Texas Conference were welcomed across the division, and the seminar approach spread like wildfire.

Evangelist Mark Finley had already experimented with "sequenced" seminars in order to reach the unchurched urban masses of the northeastern United States. Preceding his crusades with cooking schools, stress seminars, and less doctrinal Bible classes greatly increased the number of people he was able to reach.[2] Russ Potter formed a self-supporting publishing house to distribute

Finley's Daniel Seminar which, unlike Robinson's material, focused on introductory Bible study and not a full presentation of the Adventist message. Soon Concerned Communications was offering a full range of kits containing all the information and supplies necessary for a pastor or lay leader to present professional, up-to-date seminars on weight control, nutrition, coping with stress, time management, parenting, and getting to know God, as well as a seminar on Revelation, a full-message evangelistic series, and topics designed to nurture and train new church members. More than half of the NAD pastors have ordered materials, and many have used them successfully.

Finley's vision for reaching large cities resulted in his being called to establish the Lake Union Soul-winning Institute in Chicago in which seminary students could learn the sequenced seminars approach and help plant new congregations. And in so doing, a permanent mission outreach was established to one of North America's largest metropolitan areas. Eventually it became the North American Division Evangelism Institute and set the standard of on-the-job evangelistic training as a part of the graduate education of all Adventist pastors.

As approaches and materials proliferated, Philip Follett and Ralph Martin from the Northern California Conference started looking for a way to empower congregations to set their own goals and develop their own local strategies—picking and choosing from alternative methods. They began teaching their pastors a framework for planning and action called "the Caring Church strategy." It included a number of church growth concepts from such Protestant researchers as Win Arn, Lyle Schaller, and John Savage, organized around a framework taken from the New Testament and the writings of Ellen White. Robert Dale and Tom Ashlock from the NAD staff saw this as a new paradigm for the denomination's approach to the local church and arranged for a presentation to the union conference presidents. As a result, in 1982 and 1983 Caring Church seminars were conducted at union or local conference workers' meetings across most of the division. A new vocabulary of "awareness activities, entry events, and pathways" was introduced. Now pastors had a way for each congregation to develop its own unique outreach appropriate to the felt needs of its community.

By 1986 the yeast of innovation had even touched the conservative businessmen of the Association of Adventist Services and Industries (ASI). A $1 million gift was dedicated for a research and development project called Harvest 90 Adventist Research Taskforce (HART). Tom Mostert began assembling the fledgling research and development operation while president of the Southeastern California Conference and continued as chairman of the board after he was elected Pacific Union Conference president. Fulltime project directors were hired, and state-of-the-art experimentation began with the development of materials for the unchurched, small group ministries, friendship evangelism, and tools for motivating church members to witness and to follow up media interests.

The General Conference asked the world divisions of the denomination to prepare a "Global Strategy" for the 1990 GC session. The NAD officers and union conference presidents responded with a strategy statement for the 1990s, which was officially adopted at the 1989 year-end meeting of the NAD committee. The statement specifically targets the baby boom generation, highly responsive ethnic minorities, and the large metropolitan areas as the primary foci for evangelization. It intentionally commits the North American Division to "a relational approach to evangelism" and to church planting projects. It anticipates a continued process of change and redoubled efforts to keep the local church central in all denominational activities.

All of these developments make greater sense when understood from the perspective of history. What emerges is nothing less than the third era of Adventist evangelism.

The Era of Prophetic Evangelism

The first era of Adventist evangelism can be called the period of prophetic evangelism. It was characterized by an emphasis on the Word of God and a prophetic critique of the established "apostate" churches. Targets included such social institutions as slavery, the alcohol industry, and accepted norms of dress and diet. Preaching was the key method used in this era—the "period of ... the great Adventist camp meeting..., concurrent with Moody's popularization of revivalism."[3] This was a period of tremendous church growth, from 5,440 members in 1870 to 75,000 members at the turn of the century—an annual growth rate of 4.6 percent.

A major feature of this period was the great hero evangelist— men such as James White, J. N. Loughborough, A. T. Jones, E. J. Waggoner, and D. M. Canright. Their personalities, opinions, debates, and spiritual ups and downs determined much of the strategy, success, and failure of Adventist evangelism during the decades they dominated. In many ways the Adventist mission and movement was the personal property of these larger-than-life pioneers.

The primary focus of Adventist evangelism during this first era was church planting. Everywhere the camp meeting tents were pitched or city missions established, the goal was to raise up a new congregation and build "a memorial" or presence for the third angel's message in that place. More than 1,500 local churches were organized during this time.

The Era of Institutional Evangelism

By 1900 tent meetings, although conducted extensively, were relatively ineffective, notes Howard B. Weeks, historian of Adventist evangelism. (See Figure 1.) They "were characterized more by small group teaching than by evangelistic oratory before large audiences."[4]

"For example, in 1899, three series of tent meetings held in Clinton, Midway, and Fayette, Missouri, produced a total of only 27 converts. A meeting of several months' duration in Cardiff, Alabama, produced five converts. Ten separate tent meetings in Oklahoma over a period of five months in 1900 yielded a total of

Figure 1–Decadal Church Growth Rates
North American Division

only 75 converts. In Omaha, as a result of a three-month campaign, five persons were baptized. Among many conducted, few meetings produced better results than these. Tent evangelists generally seemed not to expect great things, often seemed pleased with small results, and usually attributed their lack of greater success to Satanic opposition stirred up by a stern and demanding message."[5]

Weeks documents at length how increasing urbanization and immigration had created a different context in North America that required a new strategy for evangelization. Ellen White responded to this with a plea for reorganization of the denomination and an aggressive plan for urban ministry. The development of Adventist hospitals, publishing houses, and schools was to be coordinated with large-scale public efforts in large metropolitan areas for a total evangelistic impact on urban masses.

The changes were not without difficulty. Such early adopters of the innovations as E. E. Franke and W. W. Simpson burned themselves out. Major confrontations developed with institutional leaders such as Dr. J. H. Kellogg. Not even A. G. Daniells, Ellen G. White's protégé and general manager of the period of transition, implemented changes as fast as her prophetic vision demanded. The breakthrough did not come until 1916, when a crusade in Pittsburgh drew more than 2,500 and doubled the Adventist membership in the city.

The focus of evangelistic preaching during this time turned to the communication of a Christ-centered system of Adventist doctrine. Evangelistic lessons and standard topic outlines became more important than the oratory itself. The church as an organization became more central than the personalities and opinions of key individuals. The goals of Adventist evangelism in this era were revival and the expansion of the church. In fact, the average of congregation more than tripled in size during this period—from 36 in 1900 to 110 in 1963.

There was "a growing synthesis of evangelism and institutionalism in the Adventist Church." Weeks quotes H. L. Rudy, president of the denomination in Canada, from the July 26, 1945, *Review and Herald:* "We must not forget that every branch of our work is to be an evangelistic agency. Our colporteurs going from home to home; our doctors and nurses ministering in our institutions and in private work; our teachers in our colleges, academies, and church schools; our Sabbath school officers and teachers; our laymen distributing tracts, announcements of meetings and radiobroadcasts, giving Bible studies, helping in every phase of our home missionary work—all of these are to be imbued with the spirit of evangelism."[6]

Many of the great evangelists of this period—H. M. S. Richards, A. E. Lickey, M. K. Eckenroth, J. L. Shuler, R. A. Anderson, E. E. Cleveland, Fordyce Detamore, George Vandeman, and C. D. Brooks—became the founders of such institutions as the Voice of Prophecy, Bible correspondence schools, lay witnessing training systems, evangelistic centers in London and New York, and eventually the Adventist Media Center. These men envisioned "a continuous evangelistic program" in each major city, recommending that pastors see themselves as evangelists with a four-year plan in each district they were assigned to.[7] They saw evangelism as a large-scale enterprise, with many complex, interlocking organizational elements within which every denominational employee had an assigned task.

Much as large bureaucratic industries instituted assembly lines on which each worker did one small part of the total effort, with departments supplying needed materials, so Adventist evangelism was seen as a massive machine working toward higher and higher production goals. This concept peaked in the mid-1970s with a series of division-wide campaigns: Mission '72 through Mission '77. Sophisticated packages of advertising, handout materials, sermon scripts, planning checklists, and support services were provided so that each local church could participate in much the same way that McDonald's was franchising fast-food restaurants. It proved very effective, resulting in more than 300,000 new members during that decade—the largest single body of new believers in the history of the denomination.

During this same period the evangelization of ethnic minorities—especially African Americans—began its success story. Such major Black evangelists as Charles M. Kinny, George E. Peters, A. N. Durrant, Owen Troy, Sr., J. H. Laurence, F. L. Peterson, W. W. Fordham, E. Earl Cleveland, C. E. Bradford, R. T. Hudson, C. D. Brooks, Calvin Rock, E. C. Ward, and W. C. Scales, Jr., made perhaps their greatest impact on church growth during this time. The Black membership of the North American Division grew from approximately 200 at the turn of the century to more than 200,000 in 1990. Some years the annual growth rate topped 20 percent. Today the average Black congregation in North America is significantly larger than the average White congregation and has a greater percentage of new members each year.

E. E. Cleveland "has led more than 9,000 persons to Christ," reported historian Louis B. Reynolds.[8] "Fifteen of his converts are in the Adventist ministry; more than 900 ministers have been involved in his field training seminars." In addition to founding the successful *Breath of Life* telecast, C. D. Brooks "has baptized close to 5,000 people in his ministry." Black evangelists have come to expect a far greater number of baptisms in their crusades than would be the norm for White evangelists. Although they continued to make use of large tents long after this had become rare among White evangelists, it is a mistake to view public evangelism among African Americans as holding on to a tradition or a throwback. Cleveland, for example, worked hard to build the inner-city program, always including strong social action projects in his crusades. W. C. Scales, who currently serves as Ministerial Association secretary in the NAD, includes a health fair, a Pathfinder parade, a poster contest, radio spots, health education presentations, family life enrichment, and youth activities in his crusades. He plans with the host congregations months in advance, involving them in friendship evangelism through a "kindness crusade" as well as a prayer emphasis and Bible study enrollments. He also uses telemarketing and direct mail to advertise his campaigns. Prior to his most recent crusade in Washington, D.C., about 250,000 homes were contacted by telephone.

The Dawning Era of Relational Evangelism

During the 1980s it became more and more difficult to get the cooperation of large numbers of pastors and congregations in coordinated, institutionalized evangelism. The increasing spread of different ethnic, cultural, and socioeconomic contexts in the local churches made it more difficult to build a sufficient degree of flexibility into centralized plans. As congregations expanded, aged, and grew more affluent and educated, they demanded more attention to nurture and became less interested in outreach. As North American society became more secular, it proved harder and harder to get the unchurched to respond to conventional evangelistic methods. Adventist hospitals and schools faced more competitive markets and had to innovate or go out of business. So it became more difficult for them to fit into traditional evangelistic strategies.

By 1988 half the Adventist pastors in North America were from the baby boom generation—raised on the failed war effort in Vietnam, the Watergate debacle, and the antiinstitutional spirit of their contemporaries. Adventist pastors today are far more cynical about the capacity of large organizations to achieve meaningful goals than any previous generation. They operate with more restricted resources, both in funding and volunteer manpower, than did their colleagues of the 1950s, 1960s, and 1970s. They have a greater burden to win their own generation to Christ than to add compatible individuals to the middle-aged congregations they serve.

"Today's established denominations and ministries are directed by men near retirement age and funded by donors between 50 and 70 years of age. The practical result is that their programming is shaped into a style and approach which donors over 45 will pay for and which 60-year-old men will approve."[9] Much the same situation prevails within Adventism, and the result is a slow winding down of church growth. Since 1972 there has been a steady decline in the growth rate and total number of accessions in the NAD. (See Figure 2.) In 1979 the new NAD president had sufficient foresight to understand these problems, and with the summit meeting on evangelism set in motion a process of research, experimentation, and innovation that is setting the stage for a transition no less significant or difficult than that of 1900 to 1916.

This third era of Adventist evangelization is emerging as the era of relational evangelism. It will be characterized more by an emphasis on sharing one's faith than on teaching a system of doctrines. Friendships will be the primary tool for bringing men and women to Christ and into the church. Fellowship at a personal level will be more important than large personalities or organizations. The goal will be to meet the needs of people rather than to build up institutional programs.

A relational strategy is already evident among the fast-growing Hispanic and Black churches, in which family networks are key to finding converts. And there is considerable emphasis on meeting the economic, social, and physical needs of people along with their spiritual needs. "Many Black pastors feel that much of what has been suggested as new has been a part of the Black evangelistic strategy through the years," says Harold Lee, an associate director of church ministries for the NAD. The greatest difficulty with lack of fellowship and involvement, membership apathy, and low growth are in the largely White congregations. Here exists the greatest need for a renewal of caring and inclusiveness, Holy Spirit power, and joyful worship.

At this crucial point it is important to define carefully "a relational approach to evangelism" so both its adopters and detractors can have a firm target. That is the purpose of this book. At the same time, it is impossible to write history in advance. Once an era has come to an end, it is far easier to codify its features than it is at

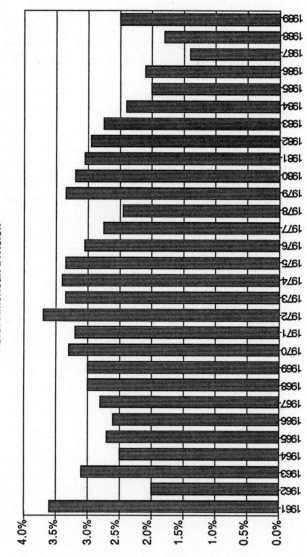

Figure 2–Yearly Church Growth Rates
North American Division

the outset. Much of the fine detail in this volume is placed here to help the local pastor and lay leadership struggling with how to implement new approaches rather than to fully define relational evangelism.

It is certainly not my intention to lay down a new set of operational rules. I hope that everything I have gleaned from my own experience and that of hundreds of others and recorded here will be challenged, line by line, again and again. But please let me make one humble request: Let it be challenged by doers and innovators, not polemicists and theoreticians. I am most interested in reports of experiments that prove some item wrong or right. I want to stimulate and encourage pilot projects, creativity, and innovation.

Above all, I long for the Adventist Church to regain its prophetic voice in this era of powerful technology and overwhelming human needs, and to disciple my generation in the name of Christ. I happened to be born into the age of nuclear weapons, global pollution, AIDS, abortion, hunger, homelessness, family crisis, ghastly affluence, and institutionalized evil. With my contemporaries, I am struggling to keep pace with the vast flow of information, the mobility and fragmentation, the speed at which change is happening, the pressure of time. I trust in a Lord that loved me enough to die for me and extends the hope of a globe cleansed of disease and corruption, injustice and killing. I want to find a way to powerfully share that unbelievable hope with those who happen to be my contemporaries. "And this gospel of the kingdom will be preached in the whole world as a testimony to all nations, and then the end will come" (Matt. 24:14, NIV). Even so, come, Lord Jesus!

---

1. The most important information of the many studies completed by the Institute of Church Ministry has been published in Roger L. Dudley and Des Cummings, Jr., *Adventures in Church Growth* (Hagerstown, Md.: Review and Herald Pub. Assn., 1983); Roger L. Dudley, ed., *A Manual for Church Growth Consulting* (Berrien Springs, Mich.: Institute of Church Ministry, 1987); Kermit Netteburg et al., *The North*

American Division Marketing Program, vols. 1 and 2 (Berrien Springs, Mich.: Institute of Church Ministry, 1986-1988); and Roger Dudley and Clarence Gruesbeck, *Plant a Church, Reap a Harvest* (Boise, Idaho: Pacific Press Pub. Assn., 1990).

2. Finley has more recently described his approach in detail in *Padded Pews or Open Doors* (Boise, Idaho: Pacific Press Pub. Assn., 1988).

3. Howard B. Weeks, *Adventist Evangelism in the Twentieth Century* (Washington, D.C.: Review and Herald Pub. Assn., 1969), pp. 13, 14.

4. *Ibid.*, p. 15.

5. *Ibid.*

6. *Ibid.*, p. 222.

7. *Ibid.*, p. 224.

8. Louis B. Reynolds, *We Have Tomorrow* (Hagerstown, Md.: Review and Herald Pub. Assn., 1984), pp. 262, 263.

9. Bill Patton, "Reaching American Baby Boomers," *Urban Mission*, 7:2, November 1989, p. 15.

CHAPTER 1
Is the Message
Getting Through?

I DON'T REALLY know anything about the Adventist Church. How do you get an invitation to attend?" For a few seconds I couldn't think of anything to say. Here I was, training a group of volunteers from a small church in the Midwest to conduct telephone surveys to identify community awareness and attitudes toward the church. The startling answer I had just received obviously indicated a woman who wanted to know more about the church.

"You don't have to have an invitation," I said. "Just stop by any Saturday morning and see what it's like." I gave her the address of the church in that town and continued the interview. Our purpose that day was not to find interested people, but to gather information.

I should have been prepared, but then came a more startling answer. One of the last questions the telephone survey asks people is if they have any Adventist relatives. "Yes," said the talkative lady, "my sister."

"Does she live nearby?" I ad-libbed.

"Yes."

"How long has she been an Adventist?" I was way off the script now, but I really was curious.

"About 30 years, I think."

All my objectivity evaporated. Sucking in my breath, I urged the woman, "Just go and see if it's something you might like."

The survey experience shocked the entire congregation. For nearly 100 years there had been an Adventist church in that town of about 30,000, and they were convinced that evangelism was futile because of prejudice. "Everybody has his or her own church, and they are all prejudiced toward Adventists. No one will come to any religious meetings."

The 317 random telephone surveys presented a far different picture. Nearly 95 percent knew of the Seventh-day Adventist Church, but only one in five knew anything about it.

There were virtually no negative attitudes toward the Adventist Church. Three out of four would advise a friend who was interested to go ahead and join it. Two thirds saw us as "a Protestant church, just like any other denomination." And 40 percent indicated they were not presently active in any church.

Public Perceptions of the Adventist Church

Four major awareness studies of the Adventist Church were completed in 1986 and 1987 for the North American Division. All used telephone interviews. The samples total more than 3,000 and were conducted by such respected public opinion and market research firms as the Gallup poll, Frank N. Magid Associates, Advance Marketing Group, and Mark Baldassare and Associates.

Although three out of four Americans recognize the name "Seventh-day Adventist," less than one in two knows anything specific about the church, and some of these obviously have mistaken ideas. Perhaps one in three have a somewhat positive attitude toward the church, while only 6 percent have actually attended an Adventist church or meeting.

Public awareness and positive perceptions appear to be improving, but not yet affecting church growth, attendance at public meetings, etc. The church's struggle is not with prejudice so much as public apathy and disinterest toward religion in general.

Saturday as the Sabbath is clearly the most widely held perception about the church, ranking highest in all the studies.

Different health and eating habits are also strong perceptions, especially among those already interested in these topics. Neither predispose people in a strongly positive way toward the Adventist Church.

Such perceptions as concern for the family, recognition as good people, and helpfulness to those in need are not widely held, but result in very positive attitudes toward the church. The world mission program of the church is highly respected both by members and nonmembers, as are its health programs.

Evangelical identity, the second coming of Christ, and parochial education do not receive much recognition unless the focus is narrowed to a comparison of several different churches, as was done in the Magid study.

Projecting a clear, simple image of the Adventist Church is greatly hampered by the fact that these perceptions are held by a diversely segmented public. Those most likely to know about the Adventist Church are the least likely to join it—people over 50 years of age; Westerners and Midwesterners; the college-educated; households with yearly incomes over $50,000; and those with professional and managerial occupations.

Half the respondents who say either that they have never heard of the Adventist Church or that they know nothing about it are made up predominantly of adults under 50 years of age; Easterners; people with little education; low-income households; and blue-collar occupations. These are people very typical of the population of a city such as Cleveland or Pittsburgh, where the density of Adventist Church members is less than just about any mission land of the Southern Hemisphere.

Are We Communicating?

The conversation I had with the woman I surveyed over the phone reminded me of another conversation 18 years earlier. I was a student missionary with the Adventist Collegiate Taskforce (ACT) in southern California and was using a religious interest questionnaire to interview Tom Parker, 35, a machine operator in an aircraft plant. His two children—Vickie, 8, and Jimmy, 10— had attended a day camp. I had visited the Parker home several times.

"I could be a Christian if it weren't for my neighbor," Tom told me in a straightforward tone of voice. How could a neighbor keep him from Christ? I asked for details.

The person who lived next door was a good neighbor—always helpful, cheerful, and ready to give free sermons. Tom gave me the following account:

"Take Saturday, for example. I was out mowing my lawn. When my neighbor and his family came home from church, we stopped to chat.

" 'Hi, what's new?' I asked.

" 'Nothing,' said my neighbor, 'except the good news that Christ died to save sinners, and that sure includes you.'

" 'That's new? You've been playing that line for 10 years. Like a stuck record.'

" 'Yeah, well, the only thing new would be if you'd listen to it for a change,' said my neighbor, then he added, 'Beware lest thou forget the Lord.'

" 'You can forget it as far as I'm concerned,' I told him, and tried to start a conversation on something else—the weather, sports, Vietnam.

"But my neighbor kept clobbering me with stuff from the Bible, such as the mark of the beast and the wicked being burned up.

"Well, he got through to me, all right. I was mad. So I said, 'Look, if you care so much about my soul, where were you when I was looking for a job last year?'

" 'I was busy,' my neighbor answered. 'You know, between my job and the church and my Bible study group, I'm pretty tied down.'

" 'Yeah, if I know you, you were busy taking care of yourself, that's what. And I needed help, but did you come to help me? No.

You didn't care.'

" 'Care? Of course I care. Why, I've warned you what the Bible says again and again.'

" 'Sure, you've told me you care, but show me,' I insisted. 'Even I can see the difference.' "

Proclaiming the message? Yes, in a way. That Adventist was preaching, but it was not the good news. A message was getting through. In fact, the medium—the Adventist himself—was the only message his neighbor was getting.

Such evangelism, so divorced from human need and so unrelated to contemporary life, not only leaves the hearer unmoved, it invites resistance by giving an untrue representation of what the gospel is. It may actually keep the hearer from ever having a chance to say yes to Jesus Christ!

Is such impersonal witnessing common among Seventh-day Adventists? Or are we like the woman who in 30 years has never invited her sister to church?

Is it because we don't care enough about people to get involved, to take the time to listen, to try to see things through his or her eyes?

Perhaps we feel safer remaining within the boundaries of our Adventist subculture or passing out the message in neat little sermons and leaflets—prepackaged by someone else. Maybe we even think this is what evangelism is all about—communicating information.

The doctrine that should precede all others, binding together into a meaningful whole all Bible truth, is the doctrine of God's extravagant love. This doctrine cannot be preached by words alone from pulpits, tracts, books, or broadcasts. The words must be made flesh where people live and struggle—in the marketplace, in the streets, and in homes (see 1 John 3:16-19).

Is the Message Abstract or Concrete?

Too often theological ideas are communicated as abstractions —unrelated to the person and his or her needs. Many secular minds are tuning out Christianity because it is presented to them as unreal and unrelated to life. So they seek to fill the spiritual void in their lives with New Age superstitions or chemical abuse. Somehow we've succeeded in making the believable unbelievable, the real unreal.

Some would say that to get out of this predicament we must discard the old message and come up with a new one. Rewrite theology, they insist, and forget about the old-fashioned concepts of sin and salvation. They talk about a "post-Christian realism" or a "demythologized Bible." Such new theology may change thought patterns, but it will not change lives.

Watered-down religion is worthless! It doesn't really help anyone. Any person who has experienced the changing, revitalizing power of Christ in his or her life cannot trade it for token beliefs.

On the other hand, there are those who say that more of the same will make a difference. They just shout louder and urge their fellow believers to work harder without considering if there is a way to work smarter. The answer, they believe, lies in putting a greater degree of zeal into the old methods and words, even if people are not listening.

These church members often indict approaches that attempt to give the good news in new ways and in nonchurchy language as not constituting "real" evangelism. "We should not bring the message down to the level of sinners," they say. "We should not pull any punches."

That kind of approach has become a classic. Be frank and earnest. Download all the truth as fast as you can. If they tune you out, that's their problem. Our job is just to warn. Never mind the results.

What Is the Future of Evangelism?

Which approach opens an effective future for the evangelization of North America? How are we to finish the work?

Why not begin with Christ's example? "Christ's method alone

will give true success in reaching the people. The Saviour mingled with men as one who desired their good. He showed His sympathy for them, ministered to their needs and won their confidence. Then He bade them, 'Follow Me.' "*

First, our Lord "mingled" with worldly men and women. He listened and observed. He became acquainted with their customs, habits, and culture. He gleaned knowledge about their inner thoughts and feelings from the music, art, and literature they produced. And always with a stance that identified Him "as one who desired their good"—proactive, compassionate, and sympathetic.

To communicate the gospel we must know two things. We must know the gospel, have a real experience in our own lives—and we must know the world, have a real knowledge of those who need the gospel.

Before we launch out in evangelization projects, we need to do research. Our efforts will be much more effective if we have a factual profile of our target audience. We need to concentrate on the growing number of the unchurched as well as the decreasing number of the church-oriented. Our personal ministry will be much more Christlike if we take the time to know more about the person we are seeking to win—his or her job, family, needs, interests, problems, and background.

Practical Ministry

Second, our Lord helped people in practical ways. He proclaimed the doctrine of love as vigorously as He preached the coming kingdom. Christ spent more time healing than preaching. He ministered to people's needs. We need to balance our use of words with practical action. For every Bible study, seminar, broadcast, and literature ministry we need an equal number of Community Services centers, family life workshops, health screening vans, and homeless shelters. Our message has no credibility apart from a visible demonstration of the quality of the new life in Christ, new relationships in the body of Christ, and a loving concern and sacrificial service on behalf of the needy.

In many retreats and training events people have asked me, "How do I get a hearing? How do I reach the secular men and women in my community?" The answer is really quite simple. By getting involved in those social-action ministries that these unreachables come to, either for help or to help by volunteering their services. I have seen the pattern work again and again. A dedicated, compassionate Adventist grandmother gives two mornings a week helping in a day-care center. She meets and becomes friendly with a young single mother who leaves her 3-year-old at the center. Soon the young mother is taking Bible studies.

A consecrated, caring Adventist realtor agrees to take on a 45-year-old warehouse foreman who is unemployed because the company is going out of business. They struggle together to get the man established in a new line of work, and together they meet the problems of family adjustment. One day the ex-foreman is in church for the first time.

Winning a Hearing for the Message

Third, Jesus won the trust of individuals. He did not simply participate in a faceless program. His service was "disinterested"—without thought of personal gain—but His love for those He served was unyielding. We must learn to build individual relationships as we do good in social action ministries and service-oriented occupations. We must reach across the barriers our society has raised between persons and mold caring relationships with those around us—unselfish, humble, patient friendships.

Follow Me

Fourth, He then invited them, "Follow Me." After Christ had demonstrated the doctrine of love, and they had accepted it and shown that they understood it by responding with their trust, *then* He asked them to admit they were sinners, accept His saving grace, and keep His commandments. He did not rush impatiently on to those important doctrines that relate the person directly to God as Lord! Rather, He selflessly waited until the right moment when these doctrines would be best appreciated.

We must follow His example. Remember, "Christ's method alone will give true success in reaching the people." We must learn the timing and flexibility that made Christ the master soul winner. We must learn how and when to concentrate on the gospel as love through our actions. But we must also learn how and when to use the wide array of media available to us to teach the full message that indeed answers the questions in hearts and minds everywhere.

When we have achieved this approach to evangelization—a relational approach—we will succeed in the work Christ has given us to do. When we begin to bring this Christlike lifestyle into our congregations, then we will see true renewal in the church.

Defining Evangelism

"It is ministry," a pastor friend responded after a presentation on Ellen White's five-step approach, "but is it evangelism?" Throughout this volume I use the terms *evangelism*, *evangelization*, *church growth*, *outreach*, and *mission*. In doing so, I risk being misunderstood, because some of these terms have been used in so many different ways that they no longer have a clear, simple, and widely shared meaning. Briefly let me define my terms.

The mission or purpose of the church is clearly stated in the Great Commission passage, Matthew 28:18-20. It begins with Christ's assumption of authority—which Ephesians 4:7-16 places in the context of His death on the cross and resurrection—and connects with the ministry of each believer, gifted by the Holy Spirit, as a part of the living, growing body. Then in verses 19 and 20 Matthew quotes Christ in an explicit command that uses four verbs. The imperative verb is "make disciples." The other three helping verbs describe elements in achieving the primary end of making disciples: "go," "baptize," "teach."

Making disciples is what Christ was about in His earthly ministry. He drew men and women to Him, loved them sincerely and deeply, and changed their lives forever. Making disciples is the clear-headed, simple purpose with which He endowed His followers. Making disciples is at once personal, spiritual, and social, because it connects the believer to Christ and to His body.

Making disciples is not simply recruiting church members, doing good, or chalking up baptisms. A disciple is one who has been born again, who has joined the fellowship of believers, who has identified his or her spiritual gifts and accepted a role in ministry compatible with those gifts. And a disciple feels a sense of being called by the Holy Spirit to that ministry without continual external motivation. Making disciples is not a short-term task, nor can it be done by mass production.

In order to make disciples we must "go." To go is what we refer to today as "outreach." It is to go to where people live, crossing both geographic and social boundaries to be present with those whom we would disciple. Outreach is a ministry of presence, service, and bridge-building. But outreach alone is not all there is to making disciples.

In order to make disciples, we must "baptize." Today we call this "soulwinning," although some misuse this term to mistakenly identify with the concept of "soul" as the spiritual part of the human being. "Soulwinning" means to win people to Christ as whole persons, not just their religious allegiance. "Soul" refers to the whole personhood being led to accept Christ as Saviour and Lord. But soulwinning alone is not all there is to making disciples.

To make disciples we also must "teach." Today we call this "nurture." After a person has been brought to Christ and baptized into His body, there remains an ongoing work of spiritual formation, education, and growth to be done. The new believer needs to understand the continual work of the Holy Spirit in his life: equipping him for ministry, bringing him into community with other believers, lifting up his life in worship, enabling him to discipline himself for the great struggle with evil.

All three of these helping verbs can rightfully be termed *evangelism*, although accuracy demands that they be labeled this way only when all three of the subsidiary processes are working together to actually make disciples. *Evangelization* is a more precise term that speaks of the whole process: outreach, soul-winning, and nurture, moving in concert to make disciples for Christ. *Church growth* refers to a congregation-centered view of evangelization and means both continual maturing and multiplying of active disciples within the church.

New Testament Evangelism Is Relational

The relational nature of evangelization and church growth is implicit in every New Testament passage on the topic. In John 17 (NIV) Christ prays a priestly prayer of ordination for His followers: He sends them "into the world" (verse 18), asking that the Father "not . . . take them out of the world" (verse 15) because "I will remain in the world no longer" (verse 11), and repeatedly invokes a "oneness" or quality of relationship such as that of the Trinity (verse 22) "so that the world may believe" (verse 21)—implying that this relational quality will be ultimately persuasive to unbelievers.

Acts 2:42-47 (NIV) implicitly states that it is because the early house churches "devoted themselves to the apostles' teaching and to the fellowship, to the breaking of bread and to prayer. . . . Selling their possessions and goods, they gave to anyone as he had need. . . . They broke bread in their homes . . . , praising God. . . . And the Lord added to their number daily."

Dizzying growth is recorded, rising from 120 in Acts 1:15 to more than 3,000 in Acts 2:41 to more than 5,000 in Acts 4:4, along with "a large number of priests" (Acts 6:7, NIV), "a great number" (Acts 11:21, NIV), and "many thousands" (Acts 21:20, NIV). But it always follows a pattern demonstrated, for example, in Acts 18: Paul comes to Corinth, an unentered city, and finds a couple— Aquila and Priscilla—with whom he shares ethnicity, social standing, language, and occupation. He sets up housekeeping and livelihood with them. They accompany him as he first dialogues with those who attend the synagogue on Sabbath, both Jews and interested Greeks. Then he moves next door to plant a church in the household of Titius Justus—focusing on those who "fear God," or ethnic non-Hebrews who have come to believe in Jehovah but are unwilling, and perhaps not encouraged, to go through the painful and difficult process of becoming Jews. He stays 18 months, then travels on to Ephesus, taking Priscilla and Aquila with him to plant a church. After two years, Paul leaves the couple to pastor the new flock. They disciple Apollos, who goes on to plant a third congregation in Achaia. Aquila and Priscilla surface again in Romans 16:3 and 5, where apparently they are pastoring a fourth house church that they planted when political conditions allowed them to return to their city of origin.

The process is always one of working the networks of relationships, with careful attention to the social currents that will most quickly carry the gospel message. Paul carefully selects key cities in which the influence of the Christian faith can flow out to the countryside. Paul adapts to the culture in each province and metropolis. He targets responsive hearers among those who fear God and works to reach those with the means both to support themselves and to travel. Paul appoints elders or pastors in each small house congregation, encouraging them to plant more churches and disciple more believers and leaders.

What are the dynamic equivalents today of these Bible examples of evangelization and church growth? Can we again find the rich fellowship, vibrant spirituality, and dynamic missionary zeal of the early church? Yes, if we heed the essentials of this process: (1) a conviction that the church is for ministry; (2) a deep sense of the Holy Spirit's activity in the life of each believer; (3) attention to patterns of people flow; (4) freedom to adapt to different cultures; (5) the working of relational networks; and (6) the centrality of the house church or small group fellowship. It is a process that can reach into the secular, urbanized world of the late twentieth century and powerfully impact the life of God's people again.

-----

* Ellen G. White, *The Ministry of Healing* (Mountain View, Calif.: Pacific Press Pub. Assn., 1942), p. 143.

CHAPTER 2

Mission to a Secular World

I S NORTH America a Christian continent or a neopagan culture? When surveyed by pollsters, 95 percent of U.S. citizens say they believe in God, and 72 percent say they belong to a church or synagogue and attend regularly.

Yet when parish and synagogue leaders report their membership, the churches of America can account for no more than 49 percent of the population. And they quickly admit that one third to one half of these are dropouts who never participate in the life of the church.

Even in the polls, only 31 percent of those who claim to belong to a church and attend regularly say religion is "very important" in their lives.

What is the truth? Are the United States and Canada largely Christian nations that have already been "burned over" by generation after generation of revivalists? Or do we live in what Mennonite evangelist Alfred Krass calls a "neopagan" culture in which people pay lip service to religion but avoid any spirituality that impacts their values and behavior?

This is a crucial issue to the future of Adventist evangelism. It begins to determine what kind of strategy is needed in North America. Should we continue to start with the assumption that our audience accepts the authority of the Bible, or should we focus on Scripture illiterates? Should outreach be voiced in terms familiar to churched people, or should we make an effort to provide a non-threatening environment for the unchurched?

When the many strands of data are correlated, a mixed picture emerges. Two out of five people in North America have no real affiliation with any religion, although some may tell you they are Catholic, Methodist, or something else. Almost another third are Christians in name only. They may have their names on the books of a church somewhere, but they have become inactive. Only about one in four is an active member. The reality is that most Americans and Canadians are like my father's old office colleague, who, after questioning my father's strong commitment to Adventism, said, "I'm religious too, but I don't let it affect my life."

Unreached People Groups

Neal C. Wilson, president of the General Conference, has pointed out that we are not reaching hundreds of cultural and ethnic groups around the world. The Missions Advanced Research Center currently lists 112 people groups in the United States and Canada in which less than 20 percent of their members are affiliated with a Christian church.

The largest groups include 2.7 million Vietnamese refugees, 250,000 Indians in northwestern Ontario Province, 200,000 West Indians in Toronto, 150,000 Hindus in New York City, and 150,000 homosexuals in San Francisco. Other groups include racetrack residents, professional hockey players, hospital employees, and the homeless.

Who Are the Unchurched?

The term *unchurched* designates both the 39 percent in North America who have no religious affiliation and the 30 percent who are nominal Christians, totaling 69 percent of the 274 million residents. (See Figure 3.) The unchurched group includes more men, younger persons, East and West Coast residents, and single adults. By contrast, the active church member group includes more women, older persons, and residents of the Midwest and the South.

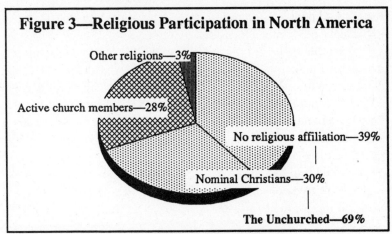

Figure 3—Religious Participation in North America

Other religions—3%

Active church members—28%

No religious affiliation—39%

Nominal Christians—30%

The Unchurched—69%

Figure 3—Source: American Institute of Church Growth

Christo-pagan is sometimes used to describe the secular yet formally religious culture that dominates North America today. A culture in which religion is defined as entirely private and therefore unrelated to public issues, business or professional behavior, and common values.

Jard DeVille, a Christian psychologist, says that secular culture operates on the basis of two principles that effectively replace the biblical golden rule. The first is "If it feels good, do it." The second is "If it is to your advantage, control it." Mental health professionals have noticed that in recent decades narcissists—self-centered, self-pitying persons—have become the dominant type of patient, and in the book *The Culture of Narcissism,* Christopher Lasch relates this trend to the development of a secular culture in North America.

People who operate on self-gratifying principles avoid getting closely involved with others. They fear becoming emotionally dependent and find it easier to handle instantaneous intimacy than deep, long-term commitments. Many are sexually promiscuous and use psychoactive substances regularly. They often express a sense of inner emptiness and dissatisfaction with their lives. They tend to crave vivid emotional experiences and feel that others should provide gratification for them, yet they have little interest in helping others. They are terrified of growing old and of death. As a consequence, it is very difficult to interest the unchurched in any type of church-related activity. He is distrustful of the institutional church and uncomfortable with organized religion, although he has a real spiritual hunger. In fact, a 1989 survey by the Barna Research Group indicates that as many as one third of the unchurched would consider visiting a religious event under certain conditions.

"The unchurched today are, by many measures, more religious than they were a decade ago," states George Gallup in comparing studies done by the Princeton Religion Research Center in 1978 and 1988. Although his surveys consistently give a more conservative picture of American public opinion than the other researchers, they do indicate that 72 percent of the unchurched believe Jesus is God or the Son of God, 63 percent believe the Bible is the literal or inspired Word of God, and 44 percent say they once made a commitment to Christ. Gallup also shows that the unchurched are less active than the churched in nonreligious civic, social, and charitable activities. While 35 percent of church members are active or very active in community events of a nonreligious nature, only 14 percent of the unchurched report the same level of involvements. The majority of the unchurched say they are not active at all in civic, recreational, or charitable programs.[1]

The unchurched are not so much hostile toward Christian ideas as they are uninitiated and disinterested in the kinds of activities that are characteristic of churches and church-related programs. For example, when Gallup's interviewers asked the unchurched, "Are there any programs in which you or someone in your immediate family might be interested in participating?" the largest number mentioned summer activities for children and youth, programs for meeting human needs, family-oriented dinners and outings, recreation and camping programs, youth groups, and "a place where we could go for emergency needs." Less than 20 percent mentioned prayer meetings and Sunday school, and less than 10 percent stated an interest in weekend spiritual retreats and neighborhood Bible study groups.

Bill Hybels is an evangelical pastor who founded Willow Creek Community church in a suburb of Chicago in 1975 with the express purpose of reaching out to the unchurched. He began with 125 core members and a door-to-door survey in the neighborhood. "Most nonchurched people we talked to," remembers Hybels, "said that church is boring, predictable, and irrelevant." The unchurched "do not want to be asked to say, sing, sign, or give anything." When they visit a church they "are confused by unwritten rules about when to sit and stand." Hybels "took this information very seriously" and designed a Sunday service that would "provide a nonthreatening environment for those who wish to investigate the claims of Christ" and make it possible "to establish significant relationships with nonchurched people." Today he has more than 6,000 members.

When you visit Willow Creek, no one will ask your name, give you a name tag or other device to wear, or ask you to fill out a card. You won't be asked to sign a guestbook, to stand, or even raise your hand. "Our church has visitors each week who are Jewish, Catholic, Hindu, or completely unchurched," says associate pastor Don Cousins. "Many of these first-timers are uncomfortable with even our basic songs and prayers, not to mention the suspicion that they might be asked to speak or to find a Bible verse." So public prayers are simple, basic, and conversational, using everyday language. Worship leaders are relaxed and somewhat informal, making use of appropriate humor and trying to project a feeling of warmth. The service is focused on the need for creativity. "If you traditionally start slowly or tend to get the announcements out of the way first," says Cousins, "it is hard to pick up the momentum. We try to start strong, usually with music, and then vary the intensity level. It's better to do a few things well than a lot of things poorly."

Lifestyle Clusters

Among which groups in North America has the Adventist message been most readily received? And which groups have been neglected?

In a study completed in 1987 by the Institute of Church Ministry at Andrews University, a careful analysis was done of 47 "lifestyle clusters" that describe the population of the U.S. The number of Adventists in each cluster was identified, as well as the number of persons baptized over 18 years of age from each cluster during 1982 and 1983. In no cluster is the Adventist membership more than   percent of the population.

In further analyzing the data, the research team divided the 47 clusters into four categories, according to the comparative level of Adventist membership and recent baptisms. (See Figure 4.) Seventeen clusters representing about a third of the U.S. households are listed as "tried and true," because both membership and baptisms were above average. These are the kinds of people with whom our conventional evangelistic activities are most effective.

Five clusters fall into the "newly found" category, in which membership is below average but recent baptisms are above average. This category represents 11 percent of the U.S. households and are the areas in which Adventist evangelism is most successful right now. Many of these people are immigrants, and most are poor. These are the people groups that feed the fast-growing Hispanic, West Indian, and Asian congregations in Los Angeles, New York City, Miami, Toronto, and Montreal.

Three clusters make up the "losing ground" category in which membership is above average, but baptisms have fallen below average. And 22 clusters with 46 percent of all U.S. households fall into the "unplowed ground" category—a major portion of those unreached by Adventism.

These unreached lifestyle clusters tend to have higher incomes and more education, and include a greater number of professionals. Fewer blue-collar workers, households with children, and minorities are found here than in the "tried and true" and "newly found" clusters. These are the kinds of people who are more likely to be unchurched and have a more secular outlook on life. They represent a vast, new mission field for Adventist evangelism.

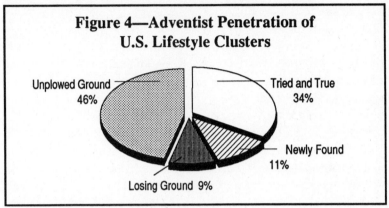

Figure 4—Adventist Penetration of U.S. Lifestyle Clusters

Figure 4—Source: *NAD Marketing Program,* vol. 1.

A Case Study in Quebec

Secularization can create an open door to hard-to-reach people groups. For example, over the past 100 years the 7.5 million indigenous French-speaking persons in Canada—the Acadien-Quebecois people—have been resistant to the Adventist message. In 1977 there was only one Quebecois baptism. But in recent years an enormous turnaround has occurred. In 1985 more than 100 Quebecois were baptized. Quebec has become the fastest-growing conference in North America.

Tom LeBlanc, director of the Project Acadien-Quebecois, says that the new opening for Adventism is largely the result of young adults who are dropouts from established churches and have begun to look around for something better than secularism. If the process of secularization had not come into Quebec over the past two or three decades, we would probably still be closed out.

Challenges and Opportunities

The Adventist message has been proclaimed in North America for nearly 150 years, yet in a recent Gallup poll only 6 percent of the

public said they had ever attended an Adventist meeting. To reach
North America we have much work to do. And as Ellen White
predicted, that work is getting more difficult.
We are an aging church, both in terms of demographics and
organization. As I scan the union conference magazines, I see more
and more centennials celebrated by local churches. As a consequence, it becomes more difficult for us to make the adjustments
necessary in our outreach programs and make room for new people
within our fellowship.

The Caring Church strategy developed by the North American
Division is an attempt to deal with these issues. It provides a new
framework that can be used by a local church to evaluate the people
groups in its area, which groups it is reaching and not reaching, and
its capacity to assimilate and nurture new people. Although this
strategic tool is misperceived by many as simply a slogan or
promotional device, pastors and lay leaders are beginning to see its
potential for church renewal.

In a survey of attitudes toward the Caring Church strategy
completed during the summer of 1988, a third of the pastors
indicated that they understood the strategy, have bought into it, and
are attempting to implement it.[2] There were also indicators that they
are experiencing resistance and problems for which they need
support services that are not being made available. But more important, pastors said that they were confused about the meaning of
the strategy and how well understood and strongly supported it is
by denominational leadership.

Considerable effort was made in the early 1980s to communicate the new approach, and three out of five pastors reported that
they have attended a Caring Church Seminar. Four out of five
pastors say they have seen the *Caring Church Manual*. In these
telephone interviews, pastors were asked how familiar they were
with the Caring Church strategy and to respond by giving a number
from 1 to 10. The largest number of the pastors interviewed (46
percent) reported ambivalence on this question, although almost an
equal number (41 percent) reported high familiarity. Only about

one in eight reports that he considers himself to be largely unfamiliar with the strategy.

The pastors interviewed were presented with eight basic ideas and asked which ones they identified with the Caring Church. Half identified the Caring Church concept as an attitude of love and acceptance. A third identified with one of three result-oriented goals: meeting needs in the community (18 percent), nurturing church members (16 percent), or reclaiming dropouts (2 percent). Only 14 percent identified it as a strategy for local church growth and ministry. No pastor saw it as a plan for increasing baptisms.

There is a high level of acceptance of the Caring Church theme among pastors in North America, but obviously a great deal of uncertainty as to what it means. This kind of ambivalence is often the result of dissonance in the communication effort, or "mixed messages." These mixed messages may result from leadership either "not singing off the same page" or using body language that contradicts their words. This may be individual body language or institutional body language. (An example of institutional body language that contradicts the message given by leadership would be the failure to bring departmental programs into line with the Caring Church strategy or a lack of strong visibility for the Caring Church categories in the publications of the organization.) The efforts of denominational publicists to date have not clearly communicated the Caring Church strategy, perhaps because the journalists themselves have not taken the time to understand it, but have perceived it as another slogan or campaign that will pass from the scene and be replaced by new leadership in a few years.

At the same time a significant number of pastors (42 percent) understand that the purpose of the new concept is to clarify and focus plans and programs in the local church so its ministry will be more effective. A solid core of pastors have begun to learn and make use of the Caring Church strategy; perhaps as many as 1,500 are convinced and committed. At the same time a larger number either do not really understand what the Caring Church strategy is all about or have an emotional block that keeps them from hearing the message.

Measured against the typical market penetration time of major new technology in American business today, this can be seen as relatively good progress in introducing an innovative approach to church ministry. There is danger that church leadership may prematurely evaluate the Caring Church strategy before it has the opportunity to be fully understood and tried by the pastors and churches in the NAD. Much more can be done in order to bring wider acceptance of the Caring Church strategy and demonstrate the advantages of this strategy compared to the cost of retrenchment and confusion if a substitute plan is to be introduced.

The Caring Church strategy is an attempt to reposition Adventist outreach, soulwinning, and nurture in terms of a relational approach. It constitutes the first step in responding to today's realities—a more secular, urban, and media-driven culture.

There are new opportunities in North America today for unprecedented evangelization. But each new opportunity requires a new approach.

Moving witnessing to the workplace. During the past two decades the average workweek among Americans has increased from 40 to 49 hours, and the available free time has decreased from 27 to 17 hours per week. That means lay witnessing must move from neighborhood-based models to the arena of the workplace. Friendship evangelism skills must be developed and taught so that Adventists can effectively disciple the unchurched with whom they work.

Finding ways to successfully reach and disciple the affluent, educated, and younger adults. These are the groups that seem most resistant to Adventism and most likely to drop out of the church. The baby boom generation is returning to church. "It's clear that religion becomes more important for people as they marry and have children," says George Gallup, based on his studies of the unchurched. During the 1990s about 40 million baby boomers will have their first child, and most will think about finding a church.

How many of them will find a home in the Adventist Church? **Supporting and encouraging lay movements to reach people through small groups.** A vast opportunity exists right now for small-group evangelism among singles. Marriage Encounter is another example of how this strategy can motivate thousands of laypersons to reach out to their unchurched friends, as is the boom in home Revelation seminars and Home Bible Fellowships.

Planting new churches. This can do more to increase baptisms among White, non-Hispanic North Americans than any other single activity. What is needed is not an emphasis on rural counties, but the planting of congregations designed to reach specific lifestyle clusters within large metropolitan areas.

Much of North America remains to be reached. It is not hidden behind geographic lines, but it does involve crossing cultural and social barriers. The greatest portion of the task of evangelization is yet uncompleted in the NAD—taking the message out of church settings and into the secular workplace, the marketplace, and the home.

---

1. George Gallup, Jr., *The Unchurched American—10 Years Later* (Princeton, N.J.: Princeton Religion Research Center, 1988).
2. Monte Sahlin and Jose Chavanz Q., *A Report to the Caring Church Executive Committee: The Attitudes and Behavior of Pastors in the North American Division Toward the Caring Church Strategy* (Washington, D.C.: NAD Church Ministries, 1988).

CHAPTER 3
Friendship Evangelism:
Key to Reaching the Unchurched

T HE UNCHURCHED are not necessarily unbelievers; they just know very little about the Bible and are distrustful of organized religion. They are not against religion; they just feel that it is somebody else's hobby and not for them.

Public opinion surveys indicate that most unchurched people feel that the churches are overly concerned with organizational matters—institutional processes, fund-raising, and programs. They also see the churches as not concerned enough about social justice issues such as hunger, the homeless, unemployment, and civil rights.

Only one in three unchurched persons thinks that "the morality preached by the churches is too restrictive." Most support high morals and say that religion is very important to them, although there are significant differences in these attitudes correlated to sex, age, race, marital status, and region of the country. Women, older people, Blacks, and Southerners are more likely to feel that religion is important. Men, younger adults, singles, and people with higher education are more likely to feel that religion is not important.[1]

This means that most of the unchurched are very unlikely to participate in any religious activity or attend any public meeting sponsored by a church. The only way they can be reached is at a personal level, through a relationship with someone whom they trust and respect.

SOF-4

Friendship evangelism is simply a recognition of the fact that most people come to Christ and into the church through the ministry of Christian friends or relatives. For example, Dr. Gottfried Oosterwal says that 57 percent of those who join the Adventist Church as adult converts list Adventist friends and relatives as the most important influence in their decision for baptism, and 67 percent say this was the avenue through which they first became acquainted with the Adventist message.[2]

In our modern, high-tech society in North America there is a new hunger for "high touch" relationships. We move regularly and work in large, impersonal corporations. We stay single longer and have fewer children. And North Americans tell the pollsters that loneliness is a widespread reality. This may be a regrettable result of social change, but it is also an opportunity for ministry!

Research with recent converts indicates that the majority begin to think seriously about their spirituality and the possibility of church membership at a time of trauma or transition in their lives. In most cases, during the 6 to 12 months before they first attend church or evangelistic meetings, they have experienced a move from one community to another, a divorce or marriage, the death of a close family member, the birth of a child, the loss of a job, or some other stressful life event.[3]

Readiness to hear the gospel message comes with the awakening of significant feelings of need. And the most effective channel through which the gospel may be communicated is a trusted friend. Friendship evangelism is learning to build trustful relationships with unchurched persons in the context of secular life and then listening and watching with patience and caring for situations in which they evidence an openness to shared faith. It is what Ellen White described as "the gospel of healing and blessing and strengthening."[4]

Relational evangelization at the one-on-one level is a process that works with three elements. These three elements, or layers, build upon each other and are continuous once initiated successfully.

First, the Christian demonstrates caring and compassion through a genuine friendship that is *unconditional*—not conditioned by any behavior of the nonbeliever! I do not expect my unchurched friend to accept Christ or join the church because he or she may never do that, no matter how much I would like it. I do not expect my unchurched friend to do anything for my ego, my pocketbook, or my career. I accept him as he is.

Second, the Christian seeks to understand the needs of the unchurched friend as they are perceived by the unbelieving friend. I do not make a theological judgment or a Christian analysis of his needs, but accept his feelings as he understands them. I am aware that his needs, along with the Holy Spirit's constant effort, will eventually push him toward a readiness to hear the good news about Christ.

Third, the Christian finds opportunities to share the alternative of faith in God as something that will meet the felt needs of the unchurched friend. These openings are often brief and fragile, and they are always highly personal moments. In the lives of some, they are rare. Usually these moments occur when secular values fail to yield genuine substance and inner strength—times when secular values don't seem to work.

Listening skills are the key to this approach. When a church member really listens to another person, he is demonstrating his care about the other person's opinions, feelings, and values. Disciplined listening embodies unselfish love and compassion at a practical level. It also helps to uncover the felt needs of the nonbeliever and paves the way for an appropriate verbal witness, even to those usually resistant to religion.

Such listening skills as "active questioning," how to check out the feelings of another person, and "story listening" can be taught in a few hours of simple workshops in which church members enjoy the fellowship as they practice on one another. These are basic life skills that can improve family communication as well as help in relating to unbelievers in the secular context of work, neighborhood, and community service.

There is a beautiful example of these skills modeled by Christ in John 4. He encounters a Samaritan woman who has come to draw water at a well a mile outside of town. The conversation begins with the problem of His thirst. But the conversation quickly moves to the deep, inner thirst for love and affection tormenting this woman with her five failed marriages. He ends up using "living water" as a metaphorical expression. It carries the deep meaning of the gospel to this lonely woman, who accepts Christ as her Messiah and becomes an active witness in the town.

In fact, several early stories in John's Gospel illustrate the whole range of needs-related approaches that Christ used in ministry to people. In chapter 2 Christ's mother and her friends have a social need to enjoy a wedding feast. Christ supplies that need. In the same chapter the poor of Jerusalem have an economic need not to be exploited by the temple money-changers. Christ acts to meet that need. In chapter 3 Nicodemus has a spiritual need for deeper understanding and growth in his relationship to God. Christ recommends "new birth" as an answer to that need. In chapter 5 He meets an invalid's medical need at the Pool of Bethesda, and in chapter 6 He satisfies the physical hunger of the masses.

Through discussing and sharing real-life case studies, church members can sharpen their ability to identify the needs of others and hear opportunities for sharing gospel answers to the deep inner pain of unchurched people. To discover the best opportunity for appropriate verbal witnessing—when the "window of opportunity" is open—first invest time in listening, then ask this simple question: "Do you have any spiritual resources to help you with this?" This approach is effective even to those most opposed to religion.

Careful attention to the verbal response and body language of the unchurched friend will quickly tell the Christian if there is a readiness for sharing Christ. This sets the stage for another basic skill: verbal witness designed to meet the unique needs of each individual at the very time of the exchange. I have come to label it Option Introduction, because you are introducing faith in Christ as only one alternative that might be considered as the unchurched friend seeks to meet his needs. To make a more conclusive statement at this point would simply cause the unbeliever to back off.

For example, if an unchurched friend has just shared with me his deep inner feelings of discouragement about his career, answering my "readiness" question in a way that indicates openness, I might respond by simply saying, "Have you thought about the possibility of establishing a serious faith in Jesus? If you were to do so, that relationship would provide you with a different standard against which to measure success in your career. You would have the benefit of knowing that a life of service is more rewarding than achieving the highest positions of power."

Jesus uses this very type of verbal witness in John 4:13, 14. He tells the woman that the solution to her deep, inner thirst is "water I give" (NIV). It has the advantage of quenching thirst forever so that those who receive it "never thirst" (NIV). And it has the specific benefit of becoming in the woman "a spring of water" (NIV), or source of eternal love.

Many church members are learning to apply this model in their everyday contacts with unchurched friends, relatives, neighbors, and work associates. It not only creates a flow of prospective members into the church, but transforms the attitudes of church members concerning the secular side of their life. They begin to see the relationships they have with others as precious in the eyes of their Lord! Secular life becomes a true "vocation" under the direction of the Lord!

One man told me that he had made repeated attempts to circulate handbills for evangelistic meetings in the office in which he had worked for 20 years, finally giving up because of the offensive remarks of others. Within three months after attending a Friendship Evangelism Seminar, he was successful in inviting two of his professional colleagues to visit Sabbath worship with him, and soon they began to study the Bible. A middle-aged lady told me of an adult son who had refused to have anything to do with religion when she was converted five years earlier, but because she was able to help him see that Jesus cared about his chronic unemployment, he was willing to attend a stress seminar at the church.

Where pastors and lay leaders are able to teach friendship evangelism to the members and set up special Sabbaths when members are urged to bring their friends, church attendance greatly increases. In 1987 the North American Division Church Ministries Department began an experiment with the Friend Day concept. To date, I have received reports from more than 40 churches, large and small, that have implemented it. Attendance by nonmembers is reported to equal 25 percent to 35 percent of the church's membership. These become an immediate pool of prospects to be visited by lay Bible ministers (LBMs) and invited to small groups or seminars.

In the Friendship Evangelism Seminar we do a little exercise in which everyone is asked to write his or her name in the middle of a sheet of paper and then make three concentric circles around it. The inner circle is labeled "close friends." The next circle "work associates," and the outer circle "casual acquaintances."

Each person is given five minutes to jot down the initials of as many people as possible in each circle who, so far as they know, are not professed followers of Jesus Christ. People whom we call the *unchurched*. People who may say they believe in God, or even have some knowledge of the Bible, but are not participating in a local church of any denomination.

It is really a very simple idea that has been around a long time. Each church member in the United States and Canada has about 200 friends, relatives, neighbors, and work associates. The church member is the best agency to reach and win this network. In fact, the Bible teaches that each of us is responsible for evangelizing our network.

The gospel commission of Matthew 28:18-20 is a command to all believers in Christ. But parallel passages always condition it. When He first sends out the twelve, they are told: "Do not go among the Gentiles or enter any town of the Samaritans. Go rather to the lost sheep of Israel" (Matt. 20:5, 6, NIV), their own kin and neighbors. Later, when many of His disciples had begun to reach those outside their own community, He states that their witnessing should be first to "Jerusalem," and then to "Judea," and then to "Samaria, and to the ends of the earth" (Acts 1:8, NIV).

This concept is a very practical one for church growth and soulwinning. In recent years it has come to be called "lifestyle witnessing," or "relational evangelism," or "networking." In the North American Division we are using the title "friendship evangelism."

In pilot-testing the seminar, I have conducted this exercise with many groups across the NAD and always discovered that most of the church members have their eyes opened to new possibilities. It never fails to generate excitement and fresh, new commitment to personal evangelism.

Does your local church have a strategy to systematically encourage and support your members in "working their networks" through casual, everyday opportunities for witness? In experimenting with this approach, churches have discovered that, in addition to the skills of verbal witnessing and Bible study, an effective training program in this type of personal evangelism must include at least three elements that we have not usually included in the past: church members must learn (1) to relate to secular people in love and compassion; (2) to recognize their non-Christian friends' perceived needs; and (3) to share faith in a way that makes sense to the non-Christian.

It should be emphasized that friendship evangelism is not a replacement for the work of giving Bible studies one-on-one or in Home Bible Fellowship or Revelation Seminar programs. Friendship evangelism leads to Bible studies. If in each local congregation friendship evangelism were practiced by the majority of the members while 10 percent or 20 percent became active in LBM or other witnessing programs, a real evangelism explosion would ensue! In fact, if a church begins to use friendship evangelism but does not have one or more lay evangelism "action groups" functioning, it will not realize the harvest and may, as a result, conclude that friendship evangelism is ineffective.

Some Experiments

Friendship evangelism has been a key part of the early preparation for major public crusades conducted over the past several years by William Scales, NAD ministerial secretary. He believes that this emphasis has increased attendance, especially among the middle class and educated. But no larger experiment with friendship evangelism has been conducted than the Northeastern Conference's Friendship '87 project. It was initiated in 1986 by William McNeil while he was church growth coordinator for this large, urban Regional conference that takes in New York City, Boston, and other large Eastern cities. The project focused on encouraging church members to invite friends, relatives, work associates, neighbors, and acquaintances to small groups, midweek meetings, Sabbath school or worship.

"Many members are amazed when they discover that the most winnable people are their friends and relatives," says McNeil. "We wanted them to get involved in making friends without feeling that they must give a Bible study." The objective was to prepare people for later invitation to soulwinning activities by making 10 phone calls, making 10 friendly visits, giving the 10 tracts in the Friendship Series, and encouraging attendance at 10 church-sponsored programs. Nonmember acquaintances who had experienced about 40 such contacts were dubbed "golden friends" in order to highlight the fact that these were people who should be especially receptive to hearing the Adventist message and an invitation to join the church. The strategic goal was to mobilize the 30,000 Northeastern conference members to make and mature 1 million such contacts over an 18-month period.

Congregations were asked to appoint a number of team leaders, and these were invited to conference training events. They were then supplied with goal charts, training packages, and other consciousness-raising materials. Pastors and church boards were encouraged to schedule special Sabbaths called Friend Days and other events suitable for church members to invite their nonmember friends. In Sabbath school classes each member was handed a sheet on which to jot down lists of names, then members were encouraged week by week to talk about their contacts.

What were the results? It is difficult to get an accurate count of how many acquaintances were actually ministered to by church members, but the statistical reports show that during the three years 1986 through 1988, the Northeastern Conference averaged 1,715 baptisms per year, compared to 1,086 in 1985. An emphasis on friendship evangelism does not replace such programs as public meetings, Revelation seminars, and small groups, but it certainly enhances their impact.

Another Adventist organization that is developing the friendship evangelism concept is Re-Creation Unlimited (RU), an independent ministry based in the U.S. Northwest. Each summer about 300 volunteers staff projects in a dozen or more state parks and federal forests. They serve the government agencies that manage the parks as unpaid "activities coordinators"—posts that were held by full-time government employees prior to budget cutting in the early 1980s. RU volunteers lead hikes, present history and nature lectures, organize campfire programs, teach classes on subjects as diverse as crafts and stress control, supervise vollyball games, and conduct nondenominational worships both Saturday and Sunday mornings. And they generally make themselves available to chat, listen, and be friendly to families on vacation. Last summer this brought them into contact with more than 40,000 people; RU volunteers serve occasionally in programs attended by several hundred people, but usually in small groups and one-on-one conversations.

Because RU volunteers work under government auspices,

their witness must be nonverbal or entirely private and at the behest
of the other person. RU's policy book says emphatically that "it
does not use public facilities as forums to urge or captivate an
audience for any religious purposes or to announce dogma as
though endorsed by that government agency." RU "specifically
disclaims that the agency it is volunteering for in that location
sponsors" the worships it conducts. "The affluent middle class is
often nonresponsive to Christianity," says Fred Ramsey, an or-
dained Adventist minister who founded and directs RU. "I
searched for a common experience shared by Christians and non-
Christians in which Christians could demonstrate what it could be
like to associate with others, perhaps in the very way that Jesus
Christ would if He were here on earth." Leisure time, especially
summer vacations, provides that opportunity, but the Christian
volunteer is clearly on the "turf" of the non-Christian, and must
minister within those secular terms.

Ramsey first had these insights in the summer of 1981, while
spending some time with friends at Lake Shasta in California.
"God's timing for this dream was perfect," he remembers. The
following May he was scheduled to take a six-month leave of
absence from his pastorate in the Northern California Conference,
and he decided to use it to explore his idea. He went to the local
forest ranger and proposed that he and his family come to Lake
Shasta as volunteers for the summer. "The ranger was interested
but skeptical." When he discovered that Ramsey was a clergyman,
he said, "I'm sorry, but we can't use you." But six weeks later the
ranger wrote and requested a formal proposal. The proposal
resulted in a pilot project the next summer that involved 53
volunteers and 2,800 persons contacted.

In an intensive training lab RU volunteers are equipped with
listening and conversational skills that enable them to "incarnate
the lifestyle of Jesus in today's generation . . . so that their vocation
becomes a vehicle to share their personal faith." Much of their
ministry is very personal—just extending hospitality and neigh-

borliness in the campgrounds. "But some of the campers get so close to us," says RU volunteer David Goymer, "that they shed tears when they have to leave to go home." And they write scores of warm, positive comments in the official logbooks—comments such as, We've been coming here for the last three years. Each year your group just gets better. Keep it up! And park officials like them. "Where do you get all these volunteers?" asked the park manager at Wallowa Lake, Oregon. "They're fantastic!"

But does real sharing of the gospel happen? Paul and Marguerite Flemming tell of a typical contact. A woman in one of their group hikes became quite talkative, and they discovered a mutual interest in natural foods. They shared a copy of a book on the preventive health practices of Adventists, entitled *Six More Years,* and when the woman returned it, she asked, "What church do you folk attend?" The Flemmings answered briefly. The hiker then volunteered, "When I get back to Seattle, I'm going to look for your church. I want to attend there." Another volunteer tells of chatting with a 32-year-old mother who borrowed volleyball equipment for her family, brought them to campfires, helped in a skit, and sang for a children's church. During a potluck lunch the woman asked, "Where do you attend church?" The volunteer answered concisely, and the woman responded, "I have a friend who has begun attending the same church. Do they practice the Bible there?" Satisfied with the volunteer's answer, she declared, "I am going to ask my husband if he'll take us to your church in our town next week. Being with you folks this week has made up my mind!" Vacationers and park employees have joined the church as a result of this ministry of friendship evangelism. There are a score or more baptisms every year.

A Person-centered Approach to Ministry

Ever since Jesus asked Peter to "feed my lambs" (John 21:15-16, NIV), it has been the duty of the lay or professional disciplemaker to seek to understand and nurture the potential for growth in each person who comes under his or her care. But "meeting needs" can be a meaningless catchphrase in ministry unless there is some way to focus energy and vision on needs that have spiritual significance. The ability to understand and cooperate with the natural process of human growth is therefore central to the work of evangelization.

Figure 5—Stages in the Life Span	
Prenatal period:	conception to birth
Infancy:	birth to the end of the second week
Babyhood:	end of the second week to 2 years
Early childhood:	2 to 6 years
Late childhood:	6 to 10 years
Puberty or preadolescence:	10 to 13 years
Adolescence:	13 to 18 years
Early adulthood:	18 to 40 years
Middle age:	40 to 60 years
Old age or senescence:	60 years to death

When congregations experience a drop in attendance and seek the help of a consultant, one of the findings often has to do with the way in which the worship and other church programs are focused entirely around the interests and patterns of middle-aged or senior adults. During a consultation of this sort, I sat with a church group deeply concerned because the fine community service program they had developed over the years was endangered by a declining number of volunteers. "We just can't seem to get the younger women to come out and help," the 67-year-old leader stated bitterly. "But you won't let us bring our children with us," came the retort from a 32-year-old housewife. The leader then listed a number of reasons that it was inappropriate, in her view, to allow children to come along with volunteers in the program.

I asked if thought had been given to developing a child-care program away from the facility in which the program was conducted, perhaps in the homes of volunteers who could not get out to work at the center itself. "We simply can't spare the extra time and energy needed to organize that," stated the leader. "Some of us have been working at this for a long time; the demand for help is greater than ever, and we're tired!"

Conflict between the differing needs of people at various stages of development in the congregation can destroy the basic unity and the spirit of caring essential to success as a church. In order to prevent this, lay leaders must be helped to see that often the behavior of other church members is related to their developmental stage and not to sin. An effective parish program is carefully planned to meet the needs of people at all stages of growth and to stimulate progress toward maturity in the physical, emotional, intellectual, social, as well as the spiritual aspects of life.

Denominational resource producers are beginning to understand how crucial this is to church life. Many are shifting away from a program-centered structure to a plan organized around "people groups." For example, the new Church Ministries Department of the North American Division has staff specialists in children's ministries, youth ministries, young adult ministries, and adult ministries instead of directors for lay activities, Sabbath school, and Community Services as the denomination had for nearly 100 years. These changes are tough on denominational bureaucrats who have had to learn new ways of thinking and working, but in the long run they will be very beneficial to local churches and pastors.

Here is a simple exercise that any pastor can use to introduce the church planning group(s) to a "life stages" approach to ministry: Decide how many developmental stages you need to work with, and get two large sheets of poster paper for each. On one sheet, list the characteristic needs or developmental agenda of that life stage. On the second sheet, list the church activities that address each need. Discussion should revolve around two questions: How can we fill the gaps? and How can we make a better "fit" between needs and activities that already exist? (You may also find some activities that need to be dispensed with.)

Pastoral care and counseling issues can also relate to developmental tasks or retarded growth. For example, mid-life crises often result in family stress that is brought to the pastor for resolution. Parents who are faithful church members may ask the pastor to talk with young adult children who have declared they no longer share their parents' beliefs. Or a senior "pillar of the church" may share privately with the pastor deep feelings of fear that what he has believed in all his life is meaningless.

How can we sort out religious or theological difficulties from developmental problems? It might be counterproductive to lecture the senior member and supply him with Bible texts when he is simply expressing some of the feelings of loss that are normal at that stage of life. It could be helpful to ask the young adult if he has thought of ways to build a faith of his own, or if he is simply responding to the developmental task of acquiring a set of values. It would be easy to respond in a "preachy" manner that might cut off all opportunity to minister to a person at a critical stage in the construction of his beliefs. It is unethical to expect of people what they are not yet developmentally capable of. On the other hand, religious experience can become a source of retardation when it encourages a person to avoid new stages of maturity.

Of course, all of this is based on the assumption that we know how to listen. Beyond that, it is equally important to be able to make sense out of the material one is hearing! Developmental stages of life provide a natural, person-centered framework to organize and evaluate what is heard in friendship evangelism. It helps us to know what our task is with each person. It provides a kind of master agenda against which to evaluate every element of the church program. How will this sermon help John and Mary and Jane and Douglas at their stages of growth? Who is that seminar designed for, and how will it help them make progress in their growth? In what way will this new opportunity for volunteer service help people to grow, and where does it fit into the developmental agenda? When developmental stages are used in evangelization, a new window opens, and fresh possibilities for a truly exciting person-centered ministry come into view.

Friendship Evangelism Resources

In the past three years the NAD Church Ministries Department has coordinated the publication of several new resources for friendship evangelism in the local church:

Friend Day Packet—A complete kit from which a local church can build a Sabbath event to which all members are encouraged to bring unchurched friends, relatives, neighbors, and work associates. Included are sermon outlines, a planning checklist, sample letters of invitation, bulletin announcements, advance presentations, and clip art to create bulletins, mailers, handout packets, promotional materials, posters, etc. Available for $3 from the NAD Distribution Center, 5040 Prescott, Lincoln, NE 68506; 1-402-486-2519.

Friendship Tracts—These are colorful, brief, and related to the needs of people in today's world. They are pocket-sized with very people-oriented cover pictures, two for each topic. One is designed to reach the unchurched person who has no interest in religious reading material; the other is designed to win a person interested in spiritual things into a Bible study. Topics include parenting, marriage, grief, loneliness, etc. Available for $6.95 per hundred or $3.95 for a sample packet from Adventist Book Centers or the ABC Hotline, 1-800-253-3000.

Hurt, Healing, and Happy Again—This book by Martin Weber is designed for sharing with unchurched friends. It includes stories of many men and women who found Christ during times of trauma and transition. It is available from Adventist Book Centers.

Friendship Evangelism Seminar—Requires about 12 hours of lab learning. Can be presented in one weekend retreat or six weekly Sabbath afternoon or midweek meetings. The instructor's manual with overhead transparency masters and a video is $29.50. Learner books are $8.95. It is published by Concerned Communications and can be ordered by dialing 1-800-447-4332.

1. George Gallup, Jr., *The Unchurched American—10 Years Later* (Princeton, N.J.: Princeton Religion Research Center, 1989), p. 5.

2. *Patterns of SDA Church Growth in North America* (Berrien Springs, Mich.: Andrews University Press, 1976), p. 40. This is corroborated in a more recent and thorough piece of research by Kermit Netteburg et al., *The North American Division Marketing Program*, vol. 1 (Berrien Springs, Mich.: Institute of Church Ministry, Andrews University, 1986), p. 54.

3. *Ibid.*, pp. 49, 59, 60; Michael J. Coyner, "Why People Join: Research Into the Motivations and Events Which Lead Persons to Join Local Churches" (D.Min. dissertation, Drew University, 1980), pp. 51-54.

4. Ellen G. White, *Counsels on Health* (Mountain View, Calif.: Pacific Press Pub. Assn., 1951), p. 533.

CHAPTER 4
Urbanization:
Can City Churches Grow?

URBANIZATION IS the reality driving most of the changes in our world. It is the single most pervasive and powerful trend of our era, and its development parallels the rise of Adventism.

In 1840 when the Millerite movement was gaining wide public attention, less than 3 percent of the world's population was urban. By the end of the twentieth century the majority of the world's people will be urban. North America is already 80 percent urbanized. In 1850 there was only one city on the globe with a population greater than 1 million. Today there are 250.

A significant element of urbanization is the development of a more secular society in which established religion is detached from popular culture and technical and scientific values predominate. The secular mind-set flowers in the urban setting.

Secularization is correlated to urbanization. At least two thirds of the people in the United States and Canada have no religious affiliation or do not actively participate in a church. And most of these live in urban places, concludes David Barrett in his recent study entitled "World-Class Cities and World Evangelization."[1]

After more than a century of emphasis on missions to Africa, Asia, and other Third World areas, it is difficult for many North American Christians to accept the fact that their "homeland" nations now have large populations of unreached people. Win Arn, a respected Protestant authority on church growth, says that while 50 percent of Black Africans have been reached with the gospel, only 30 percent of Black Americans have been reached. Edward Dayton reports in *Unreached Peoples* that American churches are losing 2,765,000 members per year to nominalism or unbelief.

All of this makes the world more difficult to reach with the Adventist message. It has been 100 years since the Adventist Church focused its mission on the massive populations of the large cities. And as urbanization has continued, there have been repeated exhortations and resolutions to "reach the urban masses." How are we doing? By most accounts, not very well.

Adventism comes out of the small-town and rural culture of nineteenth-century America, and that creates barriers to understanding the task of urban mission. Certain myths about the large cities are still widely held by Adventists.

For example, a conference administrator once told me his conference did not really need to plant a congregation in one of its large cities because "that belongs to the Black conference." A quick check of census data revealed that only 40 percent of the central city in that metropolitan area was Black or Hispanic. The other 60 percent of the city constituted nearly one third of the population in that administrator's field.

Another example is that of a local elder in a good-sized suburban congregation who told me that the people in his church "really don't understand the big city" and for that reason ought to focus their missionary work on planting a new church in the next county. As we examined the membership list, we discovered that more than a dozen of the key leaders worked in downtown offices of large institutions and corporations with a major role in the life of the metropolis.

We tend to think of the city as a monolithic structure and feel that we are not part of it. Outer suburbanites usually feel they live in separate towns. Suburbanites closer to the city core usually feel that they are not city people. Both speak of city residents as "them" and often hope "they don't move into this town." Yet sociologists have long recognized the suburbs as simply a form of urbanization by which the economically able hold on to the symbols of their rural and small-town roots.

In the late 1970s and early 1980s many Adventists pointed to a trend of U.S. demographics in which migration flowed from large cities to small towns. This proved to be a short-lived trend, and most of the rural counties experiencing significant in-migration were next door to urban counties. As Ray Bakke writes in *The Urban Christian*: "There is no escape from urbanization as a process. The exodus of families and work forces results in suburban sprawl and the growth of [peripheral] small towns and villages; this represents the extension of cities and not the escape from them that many frightened and 'frightful' people have assumed." There is also no escape from the gospel imperative to evangelize urban people.

The city is not a monolith. It is not all Black and Hispanic. It is not separate from the suburbs. The large cities are mosaics of many different people groups. The metropolis is spreading out and incorporating a wide spectrum of lifestyles and neighborhoods. Churches that want to grow and thrive in this increasingly urban culture must understand and utilize these people groups in their ministry.

What Are People Groups?

A *people group* is any category of society that, because of a shared lifestyle or values, would most likely worship with its own kind. Occupation, education, age, socioeconomic class, place of residence, ethnicity, as well as family type, all contribute to the definition of people groups. These factors "shape how people interact and think about one another. This creates a wide range of people groups. For those of us involved in ministry, the recognition of people groups is not merely an academic exercise. To minister or evangelize effectively, we *have* to do so in the context of social relationships and the culture of people."[2]

One example of a people group in the U.S. is young single adults. They usually gather in certain restaurants, exercise clubs, and entertainment establishments that cater almost exclusively to their kind. They often live in apartment neighborhoods near university campuses or large corporation offices. Most Protestant congregations (including Adventists) report that very few young single adults attend church, except where the church has started a ministry focused on this particular people group.

A book published by Moody Bible Institute identifies additional groups that are essentially bypassed by the ministry of most churches, including 35 million handicapped, 10 million alcoholics, 2 million Native North Americans, and 8 or 9 million French-speaking Canadians and U.S. residents. In 1986 a Protestant seminary in Philadelphia began to catalog unreached ethnic groups in that large city. So far their students have used field interviews at cultural festivals to find 6,000 Vietnamese; 10,000 Chinese; 240,000 Russian Jews; 2,000 Laotians; and 500 Thais. "We hope to have . . . surveys of 50 or more ethnic groups in this one city," says Dr. Roger S. Greenway. "Our great concern is that this research not remain on our shelves, but will be taken by churches and mission agencies that will use the information to begin evangelistic, church-planting ministries among these people groups."[3]

Adventists are responding to the challenge of reaching ethnic groups in the large cities, as demonstrated by the organization of the first Tongan church outside of Tonga last year in Los Angeles. The church, which has 75 charter members, grew out of a group of Tongan Adventists who worshiped together regularly at the Tamarind Avenue church.[4] Not far away, the Glendale City church has two subcongregations that worship in languages other than English.

What About the White Church?

At the same time, Adventists have been slow to respond to nonethnic unreached people groups. To begin to help conference administrators and local church leaders see the need more clearly, the North American Division commissioned the marketing research program referred to in chapter 2. It is based at Andrews University, coordinated by the Institute of Church Ministry, and involves a team of experts from various disciplines. This service enables a congregation to identify the people groups in its ministry area, study the community carefully, and develop strategies based on the expressed needs of people.

Working with a corporation that specializes in collecting and analyzing demographic and consumer information, the marketing research program has developed a framework of 47 "lifestyle clusters." Each cluster describes a unique lifestyle within the total U.S. population. (See Figure 6.) Examples: younger, upwardly mobile professionals who own homes and have children (cluster 3); young, below-average-income apartment dwellers (cluster 25); and married couples living in old homes in farm areas (cluster 23). In each case these people tend to live in the same residential areas and behave in the same way in their purchasing of consumer products. Research continues to discover the values and religious behavior of each cluster.[5]

To what extent has each cluster been reached? Adventists constitute no more than 0.4 percent of any of these people groups. In some cases they make up less than one tenth of 1 percent of the group. Clearly no people group in the U.S. is saturated with the Adventist message. As I pointed out in chapter 2, many people groups lack any significant outreach designed for their unique features.

Case Studies in Pittsburgh and Cleveland

Pittsburgh well illustrates the vast range of unreached people groups in the large cities of North America. From the two Adventist churches in central Pittsburgh, it is 20 miles to the nearest churches south of the city. In between, the population totals about 800,000. Are there groups willing to move into these vast, unreached popula-

Figure 6—U.S. Lifestyle Clusters

1. Established Wealth
2. Mobile Wealthy with Children
3. Mobile Affluents with Children
4. Suburban Families with Teens
5. Established Affluence
6. Highly Mobile Young Families
7. Affluent Urban Singles
8. Older Mobile Educated Households
9. Non-urban Working Couples
10. Young Professionals
11. Small Town Families
12. Young Working Couples
13. Small Town Households with Few Children
14. Retirees and Professionals in Urban Areas
15. Stable Urban Households
16. Urban Working Couples with Children
17. Very Young Well Educated Singles
18. Working Couples
19. Young Families
20. Group Quarters—Military Camps
21. Rural Families with Children
22. Older Southerners
23. Farm Couples
24. Young Urban Ethnics
25. Young Apartment Dwellers
26. Old Rural Retirees
27. Suburban Average Income Families
28. Mobile Less Educated Families
29. Older Urban Northeasterners
30. Low Income Farmers
31. Old Low Income America
32. Low Income Single Retirees
33. Stable Blue Collar Workers
34. Rural Blue Collar Workers
35. Small Town Apartment Dwellers
36. Middle Income Hispanics
37. Average Income Families
38. Downscale Urban Retirees
39. Rustbelt Blue Collar Workers
40. Poor Single Retirees
41. Unemployed Milltown Workers
42. Southern Blue Collar Workers
43. Southern Black Families
44. Downscale Center City Blacks
45. Poor Urban Blacks
46. Poorer Hispanics
47. Poor Black Households

Source: *NAD Marketing Program*

tions in the large cities to plant congregations? Are there pastors and church boards farsighted enough to sponsor such projects?

Mayfield Heights, an inner suburb on the east side of Cleveland, is an example of an unreached urban neighborhood. The residents are largely middle-aged and older adults—families with teenagers and "empty nesters." These are mature, successful middle- and upper-middle-class people: homeowners in single-family dwellings in a stable neighborhood. Most are Italian-American and conservative Roman Catholics. Some are Jews. Not a single Seventh-day Adventist family lives in this neighborhood, although an Adventist church is located less than five miles away. The barriers to successful Adventist ministry in Mayfield Heights are not physical, but social and cultural.

Barriers to Evangelization

Social and cultural barriers are more difficult to overcome than physical barriers. Part of this greater difficulty is because social and cultural barriers are harder to see and understand. These barriers are often denied by church members, who find it easier to believe that everyone can be won to Christ in the same way they were won. To overcome physical barriers, it is only necessary to build new structures. To overcome social and cultural barriers, it is necessary to learn new ways of thinking and doing.

The urgency of reaching the large cities is even greater today than it was in 1909 when Ellen White asked in a General Conference session, "Who are carrying a burden for the large cities?" She pleaded, "O, that we might see the needs of these cities as God sees them!"[6]

David Barrett, in his study for the Southern Baptist Mission Board, reports that Christians are decreasing as a portion of all urban dwellers. "In the year 1800, 31 percent of all urban dwellers in the world were Christians. . . . By 1900, this had risen spectacularly to 69 percent. Then the tide suddenly turned. Today that proportion has dropped to 46 percent; by the year A.D. 2000, it is likely to be only 44 percent; by A.D. 2050, less than 38 percent."[7]

Urbanization creates real challenges for the church. As one urban missionary says: "It is . . . easier to minister if one's notion of ministry is to follow . . . set methods and strictly prescribed programs. . . . Learning by rote is always simpler than learning to think. Cities challenge us to define ministry in so many contexts that ministry forms cannot provide the sole basis for our level of comfort. Doing the right and Spirit-led thing will seldom mean doing the accustomed thing. We must not be content to define ministry by the actions we take or the methods we follow, apart from thinking through the needs and social settings of the groups of people to whom we are attempting to minister. Just as we do not preach verbatim the same sermon from week to week, so the expression of reaching love will be ever changing in accommodation to our better understanding of the setting in which the Spirit of God places us to minister. An unchanging Christ and gospel will be expressed in myriad new ways in faithfulness to the One who taught Paul to become 'all things to all men.' "[8]

In Revelation 7:9 and 14:6 the remnant church is described as made up from every "nation, tribe, language and people"(NIV), and having a mission to all ethnic, language, tribal, and people groups. The purpose of the Adventist Church is to reach all kinds of people, including the half of all North Americans who live in the 40 metropolitan areas with populations of 1 million or more. Reaching out to the unchurched people groups in these large cities is our mission in the 1990s!

Can It Be Done?

Can we find a way to successfully reach out and minister to the secular, urban world in which we find ourselves? Are any Adventist churches having success with new ways of evangelizing the unreached people groups of the large cities? Are there some basic principles that can be extracted from these successful projects and used in any local church or conference?

The answer is a solid *yes* to all of the above. There are a significant number of Adventist congregations that are growing and thriving in urban settings. For example, the Brooklyn church in Cleveland, Ohio, is one of the most urbanized churches in the Ohio Conference and also has one of the best growth rates. An increasing number of new congregations are being planted in urban areas, and they usually have much better results than new churches planted in small towns. The fastest-growing Black, Hispanic, and Asian congregations are located in the largest cities.

I have had the opportunity to carefully study a sample of urban Adventist churches from throughout the United States, utilizing the most sophisticated statistical tools to identify those factors most clearly related to church growth in an urban neighborhood.[9] The congregations included in this research had an average annual growth rate of 4 percent, which compares favorably with the overall growth rate for the North American Division. They averaged about 18 baptisms a year, and their average annual loss from apostasy was about six.

Using the computer data files of the Institute of Church Ministry at Andrews University, 76 churches were identified that are situated in the central city of a metropolitan area recognized by the U.S. Census Bureau as urbanized. Of these churches, 59 percent represent the majority culture in North America, 24 percent are Black, 16 percent are Hispanic, and one church is Asian. A total of 46 of the churches are located in cities with a metropolitan area population of 1 million or more, and 30 are in smaller metropolitan areas. The study asked why some urban churches grow rapidly while others grow slowly, not at all, or even decline.

Many of the factors correlated with church growth in this study are the same ones reported in the 1981 study of all types of churches in the North American Division.[10] Four key factors stand out as significant for urban churches.

Growth Factor 1—Young Adults
The urban church that can attract younger adults and bring down its average age will more likely grow than one made up

mostly of middle-aged or elderly members. The growing churches in the large cities are those that are able to activate the young urban professionals in their membership and the Adventist young people attending secular colleges and universities. A good example of this developed at the Eagle Rock church in Los Angeles. An associate pastor was hired full-time to build a new ministry—planning and conducting many kinds of activities in cooperation with young adult leaders. Soon an eager crowd of about 200 was participating each Sabbath in a young adult Sabbath school division.

Growth Factor 2—Community Services

The urban church that mobilizes a significant number of its members in community-oriented, service-type outreach can expect a good growth rate. This is the kind of program focus that brings growth to Adventist churches in the most urbanized situations. An excellent example of this can be seen in the New York van ministry. For more than 10 years the churches of the Greater New York Conference have cooperated in providing health screening, awareness advertising, health education, emergency food, and other services to more than 50,000 people a year. Today this conference has one of the best growth rates in the division.

Much current research on large cities indicates the vast amount of human need present in them: health, economic, environmental, social, emotional, and spiritual need. Congregations that respond in meaningful and authentically Christian ways to these needs will attract new members. The development of creative, authentic social action ministries that integrate soul winning are major areas in need of experimentation by Adventist congregations today.

Some may be inclined to think that community service is only relevant to church growth in ethnic minority churches, but research demonstrates this is not true. Others express the opinion that emphasis on community service outreach will attract transfer growth, but not accessions. The fallacy of this is demonstrated by the fact that this factor ranks high when it is correlated to "kingdom growth" as well as net membership growth.[11]

Growth Factor 3—Assimilation of New Members

Getting new members involved is a key to growth in urbanized areas. Since city churches draw members from many different people groups, they cannot grow unless they do a good job of holding on to converts and making them feel a part of the family of belief. An excellent example of this can be found at the Milwaukie church in Portland, Oregon, which is described in chapter 6. It has grown from an average Sabbath attendance of 140 to 1,100 in less than eight years largely as a result of the inclusive spirit of love, forgiveness, and acceptance that pervades the congregation. There is a real need for urban church programs to use listening skills to bring healing to the emotional needs of people, an element that is missing from traditional approaches to personal evangelism.

Growth Factor 4—Goal Ownership

In order for urban churches to grow, an exceptionally high percentage of the membership must buy into the growth objective and have personal soul-winning goals. The urban setting provides a high degree of autonomy and anonymity. City people value personal choice and the freedom to "do one's own thing" without the observant eye of others. Therefore, planning processes that work toward consensus and develop personal commitment on the part of church members are especially important in an urban church that wants to grow. This means that the services of a skilled consultant may be helpful at key points in the life of the church.

The Successful Urban Church

A look at the shared characteristics of all the growth indicators resulting from this analysis, including the minor ones not described here, suggests a program-centered church emphasizing involvement in church activities, enrollment at church schools, and attendance at witnessing training programs. If this is an accurate picture of the church most likely to grow in this setting, then attention needs to be given to developing churches with average attendance over 150 along with adequate staffing and facilities to have a quality program.

A particular approach that brings these elements together and addresses the many people groups that make up the large cities is called "target-group evangelism."[12] Essentially, this means that a small group of church members devote themselves to developing contact with a particular unreached people group. Each "mission group" may include only a half dozen individuals, although they will mobilize larger numbers of volunteers for certain activities. The mission group begins by simply conducting a study of the proposed target group and praying together for the leading of the Holy Spirit. The group shapes its own strategy and program, and is commissioned and supported by the local congregation as it begins to reach out in a systematic ministry *that may take months or even years to show fruit.*

A mission group may come together around a concern for single mothers, for example. It would begin to meet weekly for prayer and study, giving out assignments to interview community leaders and gather some of the available seminar resources for working mothers or single parenting. With the help of a consultant from the local conference church ministries department, the group could easily discover how many single mothers live within a given zip code area and even learn how to use direct mail and other media to communicate with these women. As "entry events" the group might sponsor periodic weekend seminars (baby-sitting provided), and as a "pathway" it might start a weekly support group or "mothers' club," in which practical advice is mingled with prayer and spiritual topics. Over a period of years this ministry might contact hundreds of single mothers in a neighborhood, providing help and support, and aiding many in establishing a commitment to Christ. Some of these women will be discipled into the Adventist Church and begin to share their new hope with others.

Large numbers of curriculum resources are being published now. They focus on a wide range of needs and integrate biblical materials in a way that is appropriate in dealing with unchurched people. Many of these are available from Adventist authors. A visit to a Christian bookstore or with a church ministries staff person will reveal resources for high-rise apartment ministry, divorce recovery, stress seminars, campus ministry, marriage enrichment, singles ministry, parenting seminars, surviving unemployment, prison ministry, and health screening. The list is almost endless.

In many cases the converts from new people groups can be assimilated into the base church, but in other cases the project will ultimately require the planting of a new church. In fact, it seems that God is calling people to plant new Adventist churches in the large cities. A study of the new congregations organized in the NAD during 1977-1984, conducted by Clarence Gruesbeck and Roger Dudley at the Institute of Church Ministry at Andrews University, has indicated that 64 percent of the new churches with the best growth rates were located in cities of 50,000 or larger. "The best potential for growth lies in planting churches in the heavily populated areas of North America," say Gruesbeck and Dudley.[13]

Among the actions of the 1980 General Conference session was a call for special attention to reaching the secular peoples in the large cities of the world. At the 1985 General Conference session, Neal C. Wilson reaffirmed "the challenge of the cities" as a major priority of the denomination.[14]

We need hundreds of lay groups in hundreds of local churches willing to launch out and experiment with new approaches to new people groups. Business as usual will result only in decline and failure. If the Adventist Church does not allocate the resources of membership, manpower, money, time, and attention that the large cities require, then it is not serious about the task of reaching every nation, tribe, language, and people group with the three angels' messages.

---

1. *Growth Report No. 13* (Pasadena, Calif.: Institute for American Church Growth, 1983).

2. Harley Schreck, "Understanding People Groups in the City," *Missions Advanced Research Center Newsletter*, March 1986, p. 7.

3. R. S. Greenway, "Who Lives in This City?" *Urban Mission*, May 1986, p. 57.

4. News release from the Southern California Conference Communication Department.

5. Kermit Netteburg et al., *The North American Division Marketing Program*, vol. 1.

6. Ellen G. White, *Testimonies for the Church*, vol. 9 (Mountain View, Calif.: Pacific Press Pub. Assn., 1948), pp. 97, 101.

7. D. B. Barrett, *World-Class Cities and World Evangelization* (Birmingham: New Hope, 1986), p. 10.

8. *Missions Advanced Research Center Newsletter*, March 1986.

9. Monte Sahlin, *A Study of Factors Relating to Urban Church Growth in the North American Division of Seventh-day Adventists* (Berrien Springs, Mich.: Institute of Church Ministry, 1986).

10. Roger Dudley and Des Cummings, Jr., *A Study of Factors Relating to Church Growth in the North American Division of Seventh-day Adventists* (Berrien Springs, Mich.: Institute of Church Ministry, Andrews University, 1981).

11. Sahlin, p. 10; Dudley & Cummings, pp. 106, 107.

12. Ralph Neighbour and Cal Thomas, *Target Group Evangelism* (Nashville: Broadman Press, 1974).

13. Clarence B. Gruesbeck and Roger Dudley, *Planting New Churches: A Study of Seventh-day Adventist Churches in the North American Division, Organized Between 1977 and 1984* (Berrien Springs, Mich.: Institute of Church Ministry, Andrews University, 1987), p. 111. Published as *Plant a Church, Reap a Harvest* (Boise, Idaho: Pacific Press Pub. Assn., 1990).

14. General Conference Bulletin, No. 1, *Adventist Review,* June 27, 1985, p. 8.

CHAPTER 5
Reaching the
Baby Boom Generation

A N EXTRAORDINARY number of children were born in
the United States and Canada from 1946 through 1964.
Because they constitute one third of the total population
and the majority of the adult population, they have a tremendous influence on organizations, values, and lifestyles in North America.
Because they are now in their 30s and 40s, that influence will be
greatly enhanced in the next two decades.

What is the impact of the baby boom on the Seventh-day
Adventist Church in North America? And more important, what
impact is the Adventist message having on baby boomers?

Four realities about the baby boom generation set it off from
previous generations—the two-income family, an unprecedented
level of education, extremes of wealth and poverty, and a much
larger number of single adults. These realities are just as true for
Adventist baby boomers as for the general population.

Profile of a Generation

By 1995 two thirds of households headed by baby boomers will
be married couples, and 80 percent of these couples will be raising
children. "From the outside, the baby boomers will look like they
are following traditions laid down by their parents and grandparents. From the inside, however, nothing will be exactly as it used
to be," says Cheryl Russell, editor of *American Demographics*.

Sixty-five percent of married couples younger than age 55 have two breadwinners today. Only 6 percent of baby boom couples will have the traditional family of a breadwinner father, housewife mother, and two or more children. More than half of American women work, but among baby boom women, fully 70 percent are working. Nearly half the women in the baby boom generation are back at work by their child's first birthday. There is no evidence that Adventist baby boomers are bucking the trend.

Some will say that this is happening because of "a secular ideology of women's liberation." In fact, the traditional American value of owning a home is the real reason. Sixty-nine percent of couples buying their first home in 1985 needed two incomes to have the mortgage approved by the bank.

"The disappearance of the institution of the housewife has been so rapid and profound that many American businesses, churches, and volunteer organizations have been caught between statistics and instincts," reports Russell. Fewer than 11 percent of women today are the stereotypical housewife—married, not working, raising children—and this can be seen in any Adventist congregation in North America in which the nominating committee struggles to find leaders for the children's divisions. The Dorcas Society has become a senior citizen's group, and more and more volunteer jobs go unfilled.

The exceptional level of education among baby boomers creates important differences between them and older generations. Men born between 1947 and 1951 are the best educated people in North American history, and our society has become more pluralistic as a result.

Two thirds of Adventist baby boomers hold professional, managerial, and white-collar jobs. That is twice the proportion of their parents' generation.

A major goal of postwar parents was to see that their children got an education, and Adventist parents worked even harder at this goal than did their generational cohorts outside the church. One in four baby boomers are college graduates, while more than half of Adventist baby boomers have college degrees.

Baby boomers experience greater economic disparity than did their parents' generation. Nine percent of baby boom men and 14 percent of baby boom women live in poverty, but one in nine baby boom households has an income above $50,000. Adventist baby boomers are much more likely to be in low-income households with twice as many below the poverty line and only 2 percent with incomes over $50,000 a year.

A much larger share of baby boomers are single than were their parents at the same age, and this has a lot to do with the extremes of wealth and poverty. Baby boom couples have a median household income nearly three times higher than that of the 7 million Americans who are raising children alone. Upon divorce, a woman's income drops to 70 percent of its predivorce level.

More than half of all baby boom marriages will end in divorce. As soon as the baby boomers came of age, the divorce statistics went through the roof; evidence from several sources indicates that Adventist baby boomers have a divorce rate no different from their generational counterparts outside the church. Singles account for nearly half of the households in most Adventist congregations in North America, although single members are more likely not to be regular attenders and therefore are not as visible.

A New Culture and Values

In order to evangelize the baby boom generation, the church must approach them as if they were a different culture, asserts Larry Gilbert of the Church Growth Institute affiliated with Jerry Falwell's Liberty Baptist Seminary in Lynchburg, Virginia. "It is difficult for us to view boomers as a separate culture because they are a part of a whole to which we belong. Thus what rings our bell should ring their bell, and what appeals to us should appeal to them. But boomers are a distinct subculture with their own practices, philosophies, and beliefs. Ministering to them therefore requires just as much diplomacy as ministering on a cross-cultural level."

The culture of the baby boomers is largely the product of their experience, which is in sharp contrast to the life experience during the formative years of their parents' generation. They belong to the first generation raised on television and rock music. They grew up in the turbulent 1960s and 1970s. Many are from divorced families, and all were exposed to the sexual revolution. They are very mobile, traveling a lot and moving often.

Baby boomers tend to value significant experiences over possessions and status. They are practical, not theoretical, and have little time for abstract theology. They value relationships highly but most have been unable to find strong, lasting partnerships or friendships. They prefer to "tell it like it is," in contrast to the previous generation, which would rather conceal true feelings behind vague allusions and indirect references. "What is tact to the previous generation is often considered dishonesty by baby boomers," says researcher Quinn Mills.

The baby boom is a more casual, less formal generation. They are very individualistic. Raised on the Vietnam War and stories such as Watergate, they are suspicious of institutional authority and tend to believe that large organizations are essentially unreliable. Their loyalty to employers, brand names, political parties, and denominations is focused on individual representatives they know personally, to the extent that it exists at all.

Baby Boomers and Religion

Three out of four baby boomers say that religion plays an important role in their lives. Young adults often reject religion, then go back to church after they marry and have children. As they move toward middle age, baby boomers are rediscovering religion, but they are slower to do this than previous generations because they are better educated than older Americans, making them less likely to be interested. In fact, they are three times as likely to be unbelievers as is their parents' generation. "Most baby boomers I have interviewed" reports Jack Simms, "describe their experience with the church and religious media as boring, irrelevant, or high-pressured." They don't like typical church music, which sounds old-fashioned and strange to them. The Adventist Church is successfully winning baby boomers. More than half of recent converts are from this generation, but we are not winning our share of the market. One third of Americans are baby boomers, but only 25 percent of Adventists are baby boomers. There are twice as many Blacks and three times as many Hispanics among Adventist baby boomers as among the general population, but only about half as many Whites.

"Now that the baby boomers are having children, many of them are returning to religious education to give their children a set of beliefs," says Russell. "But the generation's new lifestyles mean that it needs something different from religion than its parents did. The baby boomers need reassurance that the unique course they steer through turbulent times will not harm their families; they need to feel that they are OK in an ever-changing world."

This means that what we have tended to label nurture min-istries—such as family life seminars, small groups, and pastoral care—will be most important in attracting baby boomers into the Adventist Church. Rocky Gale, an evangelist in the Florida Con-ference, has developed and successfully field-tested a family semi-nar designed to parallel the highly successful Revelation Seminar. Dr. Kay Kuzma of the Family Matters ministry is writing a similar package.

The majority of Adventist baby boomers have positive at-titudes about their pastors and local churches, but compared to their parents, there are twice as many who feel that their local church is divided, and three times as many who evaluate their pastor as ineffective. Much of this negative feeling about pastors seems to revolve around a perception by baby boom Adventists that their pastoral care needs are not being met. Preaching also gets a much more enthusiastic response from the older members. The majority of Adventist baby boomers do not feel very positive about the sense of community in their congregation.

Baby boomers have a pronounced social conscience that their parents' generation finds hard to understand. Conservatives and liberals believe in equality for minorities and women, care about the environment, have a strong sense of tolerance for diversity, and are open to change. And they say that they are uncomfortable with the gulf that exists between their values and their lifestyles.

"This is a generation with a collective sense that they can do great things, yet they are leading a life right now that's fairly mundane," says pollster Patrick Caddell. One of the things they find most appealing about Adventism is its wholistic mission with equal emphasis on medical, educational, social, and spiritual ministries. Adventist baby boomers flocked into the Adventist Collegiate Taskforce and student missionary programs in the late 1960s, and today they are most supportive of the Adventist Development and Relief Agency (ADRA), the inner-city program, the *Christian Lifestyle Magazine* telecast, and health screening van ministries, such as the one in New York City.

Attitudes of Adventist Baby Boomers

The attitudes of Adventist baby boomers toward their church is key to winning their generational cohorts. The majority of active members among baby boomers were born into the church, and this is the first generation of Seventh-day Adventists anywhere about which this is true. At the same time Adventists from the baby boom generation are less involved in the church than are their parents. Ten to 20 percent fewer report that they hold a church office, engage in some type of witnessing program, get involved in Community Services, or return tithe.

In a survey of 3,483 North American church members conducted in 1985 for the Treasury Department of the General Conference, those under 50 reported that they are twice as likely as those over 50 to put their tithe somewhere else than the tithe fund in their local church. One in eight reported that he or she does this occasionally or regularly. They were also twice as likely to disagree with the ways the denomination allocates the tithe funds.

Many baby boom Adventists simply give a smaller portion of their income to the church. In the same poll they were twice as likely to say that they compute their tithe on after-tax income instead of pre-tax income. The majority of the older generation reported that they give 5 percent to 10 percent of their income to freewill offerings in addition to tithe, but the majority of the younger generation reported that they give less than 5 percent of their income to offerings.

And this is not because their giving is being channeled to independent ministries. They reported that they are half as likely as their parents' generation of church members to be regular donors to the Quiet Hour and other such organizations.

Part of the reason for the slippage in financial support from Adventist baby boomers is the cynicism about large organizations, which is characteristic of this generation. While the majority of North American members over 50 strongly agreed that denominational "policies for the reception and distribution of tithe and offerings are fair and equitable," only a third of those under 50 felt the same way.

At the same time, it is true that most baby boomers feel a greater financial pinch than do older generations. Their incomes will never be much to brag about, especially compared to what their fathers made. Between 1950 and 1970, men's median income rose 54 percent after adjusting for inflation. The average man was making nearly $7,000 more in 1970 than in 1950. Since 1970, however, men's median income has fallen 13 percent when adjusted for inflation. Yet the average monthly mortgage payment for people who bought a home in 1979 is less than $450. For those who are buying a home today, it approaches $900.

Baby boom Adventists are not as involved in personal witnessing as older church members. They are half as likely to feel prepared to witness as previous generations, and less likely than their parents' generation to have many non-Adventist friends, help their neighbors with their personal problems, and witness in everyday life. However, they attend witnessing training events at the same rate as older members—about one in four has attended within 12 months—and report the same level of results in terms of people brought into the church. This leads to the conclusion that they must be reaching out in nontraditional ways.

Baby boom Adventists are just as concerned about the mission of the church as are previous generations, but much less likely to be doing something about it. Where three out of four of their parents' generation pray daily for the conversion of specific people and give financial support for local soul-winning activities, less than half the baby boomers do so. White baby boomers are especially pessimistic about evangelism. Only 13 percent would rate their congregation strongly as a soul-winning church, and they are less likely than any other group to believe that their pastor places top priority on soul winning.

Spirituality is weaker among Adventist baby boomers than it is among their parents' generation. Half as many report an intimate relationship with Christ or that they are "very certain of eternal life," and they are much less likely to report daily personal Bible study and regular reading from the writings of Ellen White.

Baby boom Adventists are less likely to have family worship than previous generations. In fact, the number of families having daily worship has declined by one quarter since their parents' generation.

The problems we face in reclaiming the involvement of our own baby boomers are the same problems we face in winning baby boomers into the church. We must learn to separate the third angel's message from the culture of previous generations and relate it powerfully to the deep spiritual needs of this generation. The future of the Adventist Church in North America is dependent upon its ability to make the adjustments in its structure and ministry that will bring a renewal of involvement among baby boom members and inspire them to win their generation to Christ.

Keys to Building a Ministry With Baby Boomers

An Adventist congregation that wants to reach out to the baby boom generation should pay special attention to young parents. Most baby boomers are unchurched until the birth of their first child. Then, for the first time, many begin to think about finding a church. Some other keys to building a successful ministry with baby boomers:

Creativity: This is the most highly skilled generation in American history, and it has a deep respect for programs that are done with artistic flair, careful planning, and a fast-paced agenda.

Quality: Because baby boomers are highly educated, they demand an unprecedented degree of quality in church activities. Sermon material, seminar content, youth and community service programs, literature and audiovisuals, must reflect scholarship in content and skill in presentation.

Social concern: Baby boomers will be attracted to a church that provides them with opportunities to become involved in combating hunger and poverty, to address social problems in the community, and to set high standards regarding equality and justice.

High touch: The size and complexity of their world makes baby boomers very concerned about privacy while needing quality relationships. They will feel more comfortable in small groups than in large meetings, and they usually define conventional door-to-door witnessing as an invasion of privacy. Some Adventist churches have had real success with small groups that meet during the lunch hour in offices and factories.

Relational skills: Learning listening skills will be more helpful in witnessing to baby boomers than writing out your personal testimony and memorizing it. A practical rationale for an Adventist doctrine will be more powerful in sharing with unchurched people than a key text.

Human needs: If you are able to show a baby boomer how becoming a serious Christian will help him deal with a concrete need in life, you will be more likely to attract him to Christ than if you give him historical facts or abstract reasons.

Person to person: The baby boom generation will be won to Christ by other baby boomers who are able to demonstrate and articulate faith in the context of friendships. Baby boom church members will become involved in church activities through networking, not through conventional large group methods of recruitment and organization.

Support groups: These are small group ministries that are aimed at specific needs and which begin with a nucleus of baby boom church members who themselves feel those needs are increasingly successful in baptizing new members. Examples include the Mothers' Ministry at the Battle Creek, Michigan, church; the women's GLOW Groups at the Corona, California, church; Adventist Singles Ministries groups in many locations; and even a cluster of Alcoholics Anonymous groups in the North Pacific Union Conference.

The information in this chapter came primarily from the following sources:

Dudley, Roger, and Annette Melgosa. *A Study of Attitudes Toward Giving Among Seventh-day Adventists in the North American Division.* Berrien Springs, Mich.: Institute of Church Ministry, Andrews University, 1985.

Harris, Lou. "How the Baby Boom Generation Is Living Now." *House & Garden,* August 1981.

Patton, Bill. "Reaching American Baby Boomers." *Urban Mission,* November 1989.

Russell, Cheryl. *100 Predictions for the Baby Boom.* New York: Plenum Press, 1987.

In addition, two special analyses were extracted from electronic data files at the Institute of Church Ministry, Andrews University, and used in this study.

CHAPTER 6

Where Are the Growing Churches of the 1990s?

I T IS generally acknowledged among church leadership that there is little or no growth among White churches in the North American Division. In 1988 a total of 31,681 people were baptized or made professions of faith. At least 16,500 of these (52 percent) were in Black, Hispanic, and other minority churches. Of the remaining 48 percent—accessions to White, Anglo churches—research indicates that about one in five was a child from an Adventist home. Only about 12,000 were adult converts—less than 4 per congregation that year.

Yet there is a handful of White churches in North America in which spectacular, sustained growth is happening. The Milwaukie church in Portland, Oregon, had 330 members in 1982. By 1989 its membership exceeded 800—a growth rate of 10 percent to 20 percent each year for seven years. Its increase in average Sabbath attendance and tithe is even greater.

When Dan Simpson became pastor of the Azure Hills church near San Bernardino, California, in 1985, the average weekly worship attendance was 400 to 500. By late 1988 an average of 1,100 people were attending three worship services each Sabbath, and in April 1989 a new congregation was spawned less than seven miles away. By the end of the year both churches had steady attendances above 1,000. Membership has gone from 1,254 in

January 1985 to 1,942 in October 1989—1,530 at Azure Hills and 412 in the new congregation. This reflects an annualized growth rate in excess of 10 percent per year. Not only do Adventist pastors within driving distance report no losses in attendance, but during this same period, campus chaplain Clarence Schilt at nearby Loma Linda University began the Chapel church—an alternative worship service that ministers to 400 or more graduate students and young adults each Sabbath.

The Arlington church near Fort Worth, Texas, grew from 300 to 500 members between 1985 and 1988. The Suburban church in Buffalo, New York, had an attendance of 70 to 80 each Sabbath in early 1984. By 1987 worship attendance averaged 175. The Norwalk church in a Los Angeles suburb has tripled its membership since 1980.

Exciting things are happening in these congregations! Each of these churches is successfully reaching out to and involving baby boomers. The Spirit is moving and showing the way for significant church growth among White, middle-class North Americans in their 20s, 30s, and 40s. It can be done!

The Milwaukie Experience

In 1982 when he moved to Portland, "Sabbath attendance was about 140," remembers David Snyder, senior pastor of the Milwaukie Seventh-day Adventist Church. "I became strongly impressed that God had a very special calling for this particular congregation." He was particularly interested in why there were thousands of nonattending and former Adventists in the city, and focused on two major problems—"worship services that did not meet spiritual needs" and "a strongly legalistic attitude," which he felt was communicated by many Adventists.

"My challenge to the church board was to look at every facet of our methodology in the light of our stated mission. I suggested we abandon anything that was merely traditional, that somehow had lost its meaning and effectiveness." Snyder concluded that "changes had to be made," especially in the worship service. "Rigid formality was ruled out and replaced with a warm, happy environment of holy celebration." Sermons were to be "biblical, Christ-centered, and relevant to the people's felt needs." Specific steps were to be taken to ensure that real fellowship happened on Sabbaths. No person in attendance, regardless of his attitude or lifestyle, would be "allowed to feel unnoticed, unwanted, or condemned."

Today average Sabbath attendance is about 1,200, and half the crowd are men and women in their 20s and 30s, "a phenomenon that is virtually unheard of in North American Adventist churches," comments Steve Daily, chaplain on the Riverside campus of Loma Linda University.

A free-lance writer who is one of the local elders describes what it is like to attend Milwaukie. "Even before I get to the door . . . one of several deacons greets me with a warm smile and handshake. . . . The cover of the weekly bulletin proclaims, 'Love, Acceptance, and Forgiveness.' And the demeanor of the people who greet me makes it clear that this is not a matter of mere words. It doesn't matter what burdens you carry. It doesn't matter what your past has been. It doesn't matter how you are dressed. We're going to love you regardless, and keep on loving you until you know our wonderful Jesus intimately.

"We have a musical group that leads out every time the family of God is together. Their ministry is an important part of our worship. Besides lead singers, there are guitars, a keyboard, piano, and a muted set of drums. Biblical? Look at 2 Chronicles 5:12-14 and Psalm 150." There is clapping, he admits—North American Adventists were startled to find at the 1985 General Conference session in New Orleans that clapping is common in some parts of the world—and recommends we look at 2 Kings 11:12 and Psalm 47:1 before condemning the practice. "We are there to celebrate, and celebration is never boring.

"Perhaps the most beautiful part of our service is the altar of prayer. Without fanfare the pastor invites us all to come forward

and kneel at the front of the church. . . . The response is immediate
and natural as people flow to the front. Those who have not chosen
to come forward that Sabbath also kneel as our musical group sings
'Someone is praying for you.' The pastor closes with a brief
congregational prayer, and all return to their seats. . . . Many
remarkable answers to prayer have come as a result of this fellowship in supplication.

"When our pastor finishes preaching, he offers a brief prayer
and says something like 'Have a blessed Sabbath. You're dis-
missed.' This is a signal for us to mingle with others in the body
of Christ. We're family, brothers and sisters. We minister to each
other and share our joys in the Lord. We also want to meet and get
acquainted with those who are new in our midst."

The ministry of Milwaukie is not limited to Sabbaths. During
the 1988-1989 program year it offered 14 weekly small groups,
eight adult Sabbath school classes, and "Praise and Preaching" on
Wednesday evenings, which attracts at least 150 people each week.
Two specialized ministries have been developed over several years:
a singles ministry called SOLOS (Singles Openly Loving Our
Saviour) and a young adult ministry called 20something.

"Our singles ministry has a weekly Bible fellowship and social
activities each month," says Snyder. "The group has grown to 150
singles between the ages of 30 and 59. Our young adult group, ages
19 to 30, has a weekly Sabbath school class, a Friday evening Bible
fellowship, and social activities each month. This group numbers
around 60 active members." Each group has a monthly newsletter.

"We have taken on another staff member who will be working
full time with our small group ministries . . . and he will work with
the senior pastor to establish a lay pastors' ministry." His title is
director of church ministries. The staff also includes an associate
pastor, and a Bible worker who is funded part-time by the local
church, as well as office and janitorial workers.

"We will be establishing a number of new ministries," says
Snyder, "and exploring new church growth concepts. We have

begun an extensive building project for a new facility to worship in." This is the second building campaign in a relatively few years. The Milwaukie congregation was forced out of a brand-new physical plant because it grew so rapidly, and is presently renting the New Hope church on Saturdays.

The Milwaukie church has a simple mission statement. Its purpose is "to (1) encourage people to accept Jesus Christ as Saviour and Lord; (2) provide an atmosphere that fosters Christian growth, fellowship, and service; (3) help people, through the power of the Holy Spirit, reach their full potential spiritually, mentally, and physically." Each of these three points is elaborated on in a brief paragraph concretely describing the kind of ministry it seeks to do to fulfill this mission. "If there is anything unique about it, it may be that it is lived rather than merely stated," says Snyder.

The change has not come about easily or been without conflict. Synder reflects that some of his original group of members "didn't like such a large group for worship, others were offended by the praise singing each week, and still others decided the church had lost its 'reverence.' Some members were unhappy with the new spirit of tolerance, and others simply didn't like this pastor who had 'ruined' their church." A number who were uncomfortable with the changes transferred their membership to other Adventist congregations in the city.

Rumors about the Milwaukie church are rife. Even in print it has been asserted that "they speak in tongues," although there is no basis in fact for that charge. "They allow people to wear jewelry," one denominational staffer was told when he moved to Portland. Sure enough, on his first visit to Milwaukie, during the greeting time, the woman with earrings sitting in front of him turned around and welcomed him to "our church." Further conversation revealed that this was only her third Sabbath in attendance, and that she came from a non-Adventist background and had not even begun Bible studies. This worker had brought an unchurched friend with his family that Sabbath for a first visit to an Adventist church, and as they were leaving, the unchurched friend scolded his teenage daughter for having lost her necklace. "I just put it away," the teenager said, and then matter-of-factly, "they don't wear jewelry here."

Any time significant numbers of people who have little under-standing of the traditional Adventist subculture begin to attend on Sabbaths, the congregation will be treated to behaviors it might not prefer. Attempts to control these behaviors among newcomers who have little or no loyalty to the organization will only result in closing the door to church growth and evangelism. Do some people in attendance at Milwaukie raise their hands during prayer and singing in the fashion of charismatics? Yes. Is this such an egregious infraction that they should be told to stop? Obviously not.

A congregation cannot arrange everything to its own level of optimum comfort and then expect to grow. "Do we allow a few vocal individuals to hinder the advancement of God's kingdom?" asks Snyder. "Had I given way to pressure, we would still be a small, self-centered group with no real goal beyond maintaining the status quo."

"There was no attempt to be novel or nonconformist but rather an earnest desire to respond to the Spirit's leading," says Oregon Conference president Don Jacobsen. "Not everyone agreed. Not everyone understood. In fact, not everyone was gracious, which is too bad, really.

"In many unimportant ways we are more different than we are alike. I think that is healthy. It does not compromise our theology, but it both gives us freedom to be unique as God has made us and also alerts us to the fact that the message we proclaim is appealing to a wide spectrum of people. It is also, however, more than a little frightening to some.

"There are some who . . . desire a different ambience in which to worship God. And if that mode does not violate any theological positions, should they be denied? It seems to me that would be as unreasonable as insisting that our Chinese believers learn English before they can become members of the Adventist family. . . . In a multichurch community . . . it would actually be restrictive to the work of the gospel if there were not some diversity."

Jacobsen says, "I am personally blessed by the ministry of the Milwaukie church," and makes four points about which he is often asked:

1. The growth of the church is not due to gimmicks or novel ideas but is a result of the congregation's commitment to follow the leading of the Holy Spirit.

2. Spirit-filled, biblical preaching is central to the program of the church.

3. A live, personal, awe-inspiring, Christ-centered praise service is itself attractive in the best sense of the word.

4. A nontraditional Sabbath morning is only one part of the Milwaukie experience. Membership at Milwaukie follows the same pattern of preparation as in every other Adventist church.

One of the concerns that are brought up repeatedly by those who are uneasy about the kind of innovation happening at Milwaukie is flagged by the term *congregationalism*. In fact, their misuse of the term reveals an unfamiliarity with its definition, but it is important to see how the Milwaukie church has specifically committed itself to strong support of the denomination. Its mission statement says, "Our church recognizes its cooperative role as a part of the Seventh-day Adventist Church worldwide." And, "we feel God has entrusted us with certain vital biblical truths that need to be shared."

Does the Milwaukie church have a strong stewardship emphasis? In 1982 its annual tithe was $140,000, and by 1988 it had grown to $375,000—an average annual increase of 28 percent in years when inflation in the United States was running about 3 percent and tithe increases across the NAD were averaging 5 percent. The tithe growth rate outpaced the membership growth rate of the congregation, and giving to the local budget is usually 45 percent to 50 percent of the tithe. That is much better than the majority of local churches across North America.

To what extent is this phenomenal growth the result of real evangelism—bringing men and women to Christ—and to what extent is it the result of transfers from other Adventist churches in the city? Since 1982 the Milwaukie church has had 20 to 40 baptisms each year—a significant increase over previous years. This may not seem like spectacular results compared to ethnic churches and those outside North America, but it is very good among White, Anglo, NAD churches. The 1988 annual report of the Oregon Conference indicates that two congregations shared honors for having the largest number of baptisms that year: Milwaukie and a Black church in Portland. "Our pastor makes it a practice never to ask anyone to join our church family if he or she is already a member in a local Adventist congregation," states one of the elders.

"Be sure God is directing before attempting any radical changes," Snyder says to fellow pastors. "But if God is leading, you dare not hold back. Even if it means facing strong opposition or shifting your place of ministry. Let me stress that the end of such progression is sweet unity. The Milwaukie family is now the most closely knit congregation I have ever known. . . . An hour after any scheduled meeting, the aisles and foyer still hold those who hate to part company and go home."

One of the elders lists several recommendations from the Milwaukie leadership to church boards considering similar innovations:

1. This kind of outreach and nurture is "based on righteousness by faith" for its theological underpinnings. It "will not thrive on a legalistic base."

2. "Don't go this route if you would rather not grow in size." Some congregations prefer to remain small.

3. "Expect a certain amount of opposition. This type of worship is a vast change from the traditional approach. Some may feel uncomfortable and transfer to a more traditional congregation,

a choice they should have."

4. "The pastor's role is crucial." Innovation requires skilled pastoral leadership. "A strong core of lay leaders who believe in the program also is essential." It must be a team effort.

5. "Let your conference president know you are Bible-oriented, doctrinally sound, loyal members of the Seventh-day Adventist Church." Innovation should not mean disloyalty in the minds of any. If conference leadership is not fully informed, they cannot provide support for the church when questions are asked and rumors floated.

6. "Accept certain behavior (such as hand raising) but don't hold that up as proof of a close relationship with God—thus relegating others to second-class citizenship in the kingdom." Mature believers should be able to accept behaviors they are unaccustomed to without finding it necessary to either censure or adopt the behaviors.

7. "In accepting all who come to worship Christ, you'll likely be accused of 'collecting garbage.' Don't argue; merely point to the ministry of Christ for the despised of His day, and to what many of them became under His blessing." This is, unfortunately, likely to happen when dropouts from other congregations in the city are reactivated in another Adventist church.

8. "Sometimes members of other denominations will want to worship with your church group regularly. We let such know that, while we would love to have them as fellow SDAs, they are welcome to worship with us as long as they wish. And we make them feel an integral part of our church family. They are not 'outsiders.' " This is an essential element in a soul-winning church.

The Azure Hills Story

"You begin to realize that something is different when you drive into the church parking lot. There are no spaces available. Not just during the 11:00 hour, but during all three services held every

Sabbath morning," wrote one visitor to the Azure Hills Seventh-day Adventist Church in mid-1988. It is located in Grand Terrace, a southern California suburb about halfway between San Bernardino and Riverside—cities of a half million population each. The 8:15 a.m. worship is a "family service" designed especially for parents with young children. "Here, while the children are fresh, is a service in which they can participate," says senior pastor Dan Simpson. It is the only one of the three services that includes a children's story. "We try to keep the music a little lighter for the children, and they collect the offering."

The 9:45 a.m. worship is for teens and young adults. "We don't just tell the youth to come and let us minister to them in the way we think they should appreciate," continues Simpson. "We try to scratch where it itches . . . a service that meets their needs, speaks to them, and sings their songs." It includes a contemporary Christian band with drums, synthesizers, and electric guitars. The senior pastor delivers the sermon nearly every week "because the youth are as important as any of the adults in the congregation."

The 11:00 a.m. worship "is our most traditional," Simpson declares, but it is still quite different than what many long-time Adventists have come to expect. "Instead of organ music and hymnals, each service features lively Christian music with the words projected on a huge, overhead screen," reports Steve Daily, chaplain at the Riverside campus of Loma Linda University. "Praise and celebration dominate the service. . . . There is a sense of involvement and participation in these services that is uncommon in Adventist worship."

Steve Gifford, president of the Southeastern California Conference, describes it as "a Black church with White people attending," referring to the fact that most Black Adventist churches in North America have always had the sense of participation and vibrancy, the lively music, and spontaneous shouts from the listening congregation that have been incorporated into the dialogic character of Black preaching. "Though our services sometimes give the feeling of spontaneity," says Simpson, "there is a plan." In fact, he and his staff work much harder to prepare these innovative worships than do pastors following a more conventional order of service.

The minister of music, "spends much time planning music themes that lead people to worship joyfully and completely. The Sabbath morning sermon is planned to lead people into a personal relationship with Jesus Christ. . . . Our 20 minutes of music celebration, where the congregation participates fully and isn't just entertained, is designed first to thrill hearts and then to lead people to an attitude of prayer for the Garden of Prayer." This feature is included in each of the worship services. It begins as one of the pastors goes to the pulpit, the music takes on a meditative flavor, and the congregation is invited forward to kneel and pray "for specific joys or burdens in their lives or the lives of others." As everyone kneels, 30 to 60 individuals move up to the wide, sloping steps in front of the platform. The elders leave the platform and are joined by other lay pastors "to lay hands on" those who have come forward. The prayer from the pulpit is somewhat longer than the norm in other Adventist churches to allow time for contact to be made by one of the lay ministers with each of the men and women kneeling in the front.

Steve Bottroff, director of creative ministries, sees all three worship services rooted in the belief that it is God's will for the human spirit to be uplifted. He often directs the use of drama to visually portray eternal truths about God and about the Christian life. These are not plays in which several actors have memorized roles, nor do they involve any backdrops, props, or costumes. They are descriptive, narrative readings by one person at the pulpit while an ensemble of a dozen people portrays stylized body language coordinated to the emotions and ideas in the reading. It is neither dance nor "holy aerobics." The movements are quiet, dignified, careful, and the group wears simple, modest, and unadorned clothing. The closest thing to these "dramas" that I have seen is a deaf choir, but it is very effective and moving.

The reason for the three worship services is not for space, but for the purpose of providing a range of worship options to a diverse congregation. The Sabbath school functions alongside both the 9:45 and 11:00 a.m. worships, and it too offers a range of choices. There is a traditional adult Sabbath school in the fellowship hall that breaks up into four classes for the lesson study. Alternative classes include the pastor's Bible class, a 12-step group for recovery from addictions, and seminars and small groups focusing on discovering spiritual gifts, total healing, principles of Christian finance, healing the family, prevailing prayer, and healing damaged emotions. A full range of age-graded divisions for children is also offered.

The Azure Hills church works to provide caring, Christ-centered ministry during the entire week as well. A growing number of lay pastors lead "TLC Groups" (tender loving care) in their homes. "They meet when people are available," says Simpson, "evenings, mornings, even Sabbath morning." Each lay pastor is responsible for gathering his or her own group around a particular need or goal. "Some are fellowship and study groups; others are special ministry groups—prayer, healing, dysfunctional families, divorce recovery, etc." On the Sabbath when I visited Azure Hills in early 1989, flyers were passed out announcing 11 new groups: four in Grand Terrace, four in Loma Linda, and one each in Redlands, Mentone, and Riverside. Included was a group on life application of the Bible, another on healing the family, and another in Spanish. The goal is to have 200 lay pastors leading groups by the end of 1990.

The church is open for prayer every morning through the week from 7:00 to 9:00 a.m. and every evening from 5:00 to 6:00 p.m. "We provide times for learning how to pray," states Simpson, "not just a 'Hello' in the morning but for long periods of time." By the end of 1990 it is his goal to have 1,000 people praying every day for the congregation and its ministries. Azure Hills also sponsors a youth center, a Pathfinder Club, a children's ministry, and counseling services.

By early 1989 the church was "facing strangulation in its present facilities." The congregation's planning committee reviewed a number of options, including building a larger facility, but recommended that several hundred members "swarm" to establish another local church nearby. In a survey of the membership, 545 indicated their willingness to join the new congregation. The Azure Hills church board and the Southeastern California Conference executive committee voted approval of the plan in February. More than 700 were in attendance for the inaugural Sabbath in April at a rented Assembly of God church in Colton, another San Bernardino suburb about seven miles from the Azure Hills location.

The new church board selected the name "Celebration Center" rather than a geographic name to emphasize its outreach to people who need a particular style of ministry. The new church will be "nontraditional but every bit Adventist," declares Simpson. This congregation has resulted from a vision of becoming a church where God's forgiveness, healing, and redemption find human expression; exploring creative ways to meet people's spiritual, emotional, and physical needs.

"A church does not just become an exciting place to worship and minister," points out Simpson. "There must be day-by-day, year-by-year planning for the future." The document voted by the church that states its vision for the future includes the goals of "a church that is committed to praying . . . to our Seventh-day Adventist pillar beliefs and world mission . . . to the loving acceptance of all people . . . to meet people's needs . . . to result in baptisms from laypeople's witness . . . to the development of its members' Spirit-given gifts . . . to a high degree of training for its elected people . . . to be a model for the denomination."

Simpson has experienced significant resistance to some of the changes, especially when the traditional adult Sabbath school was moved from the sanctuary to the fellowship hall to make room for a third worship service each Sabbath. He, like Dave Snyder in Portland, has been criticized by some who believe that any deviation from conventional forms of worship and church life is to be avoided like the plague. But he has also confronted the apathy and disengagement of the more liberal church members in his area. He is providing a successful model for meeting the challenge that faces many Adventist churches today in North America as they become white-collar congregations. "The time, energies, and priorities of church members are increasingly sucked away from volunteerism and church life," observes Daily. And "Adventists tend to be quite individualistic in their approach to life."

An Earlier Case: Garden Grove

This is not a new story. There is an earlier precedent in the Garden Grove Seventh-day Adventist Church located in Orange County, the 2-million-resident bedroom community to the south of Los Angeles. Norman Versteeg became pastor in August 1968, and in 12 years it grew from 340 members to 1,120—an annualized growth rate of about 20 percent. In an April 1981 article in *Ministry* Versteeg pointed out that he had "established an unofficial record for length of service in one church," and argued for longer tenure in pastorates.

"Give your church members the privilege of planning long-range goals with you and of working together to achieve them," he wrote. "God wants His local congregations to grow. He expects us to plan well and thoroughly, and to stay long enough to follow through our plans. He doesn't want to hear us groaning that we are a poor, unpopular, persecuted little group that can't grow." His experience with Garden Grove demonstrates that "longer pastorates . . . encourage numerical growth, long-range planning, and spiritual nurture of members" as well as "give pastors the freedom to develop a specialized ministry to meet the needs of a particular area."

Versteeg, like Snyder and Simpson, was plagued with the "small is sacred, big is bad" attitude. He told the 1980 Theological Consultation at Glacier View, "We desire to demonstrate what has not been done in our denomination. With no large institution to employ members, we desire to grow to a membership of three to five thousand . . . through evangelism and discipleship, not transfers of huge numbers of people. . . . Our objective is to become a dynamic fellowship well known in our territory."

The themes that Versteeg shared with the assembled administrators and scholars in 1980 are those that have found expression at Milwaukie, Azure Hills, and elsewhere. He said "the church must become a place of love and acceptance; the church must be challenged to grow; the church must change its concept of witnessing; the church must change its preaching emphasis; (and) the church must be sure of salvation."

Garden Grove church has a strong program of Home Bible Fellowships. "In our congregations we must provide two things," Versteeg believes. "The intimacy of a small group; a church of 14. We must also have the resources of a larger congregation. If we don't, we will be the only ones who know we're here. That isn't God's plan. . . . We could be like a thousand other churches. . . . Good little churches, rather harmless, with fine people, yet little or no growth. Pastors coming and going; short-range plans or no plans at all. Managing to survive in the world, holding their own, but not exciting anyone or even being noticed by non-Christians, surely not scaring the devil!"

Garden Grove church also sponsors a lay ministry training center for the conference. In these classes Versteeg has been teaching friendship evangelism concepts since the early 1970s. "Witnessing," he says, is "letting Jesus walk with you, then telling others about your Friend. Witnessing [is] not an occasional unpleasant activity, but a way of life."

In 1982 Versteeg swarmed with a number of the Garden Grove members to plant a new congregation in nearby Irvine—a newly developed "gold coast" suburb immortalized in the *Knots Landing* television series. It was an unreached territory for the Adventist Church and a hard-to-reach people group: the affluent, educated, and powerful. The congregation is called the Saddleback Valley church and has doubled its membership in seven years. About 180 members formed the core of the new congregation, and now has 379. The Garden Grove church is back up to 1,233 members under the new senior pastor, Keith Knoche. This case study demonstrates that this kind of church growth can have a lasting effect on expansion of the kingdom.

Why Ethnic Churches Are Growing

The spectacular growth rates at the Milwaukie and Azure Hills churches are "par for the course" among Black and Hispanic Adventist congregations in North America. "There is a temptation to give racist explanations," says Dr. Ron Graybill, a White writer on race relations. "Oh, we say, Black people are more religious, Hispanics are less well educated. These explanations may be as self-defeating as they are wrong. Not only are they ethnically belittling; they slur our beliefs by suggesting that our teachings appeal primarily to people who don't know any better or can't help themselves." And there is the concrete evidence that just because a congregation is Black or Hispanic does not automatically mean that it will grow rapidly. There are also some static and declining ethnic churches. Nor is it true that growth is related only to poor people; some of the fastest growing Black churches are predominantly middle-class.

Many examples of rapidly growing Black churches can be given. One is the United church in Decatur, a suburb of Atlanta. It began as a church-planting project in 1983 with 72 charter members and had 493 by the end of 1989. Attendance has hit 500—the physical limit of the seating and parking in the congregation's facility—says Earl W. Moore, who has been the pastor from the beginning. After more than 20 years in departmental and administrative assignments, he convinced the South Atlantic Conference president to let him pastor again. "I was part of the staff of the Review and Herald Publishing Association, and I traveled and visited churches all over North America, and what I saw time and time again was the lack of a personal relationship between the pastor and the congregation; what people want is fellowship. I just believe that Jesus is coming soon, and want the joy of being close to the people!" His philosophy of ministry is to "do what generates the most love and involvement" on the part of the people.

Moore says that United's worship probably isn't much different than what would be found in many Black Adventist churches. "We try to make it warm and compelling, and show people the beauty and joy of involvement. The members say they hate to be away." Music has always been a very important part of Black worship, and Moore says that the music used today at the United church has changed some. There is "more gospel music, although I don't let it deteriorate. . . . I want a balanced diet." And the minister of music, Harriet Taylor, knows how to put it together.

The morning prayer is a key part of Sabbath worship. Moore is one of those pastors who believe that a pastor's congregation should hear their pastor pray for them. "When I'm there, I pray." He reads the names of the sick and others who have phoned in prayer requests, and then asks anyone who has a special need to come down to the front of the sanctuary and join him. "We've removed the railing and carpeted the steps around the platform to make room for people to join in. We've had many answers to prayer," he rejoices, and 75 to 100 people get up from their seats and join him each Sabbath.

Although he does deal with personal needs, Moore says his preaching, like that of many Black pastors, is primarily prophetic. "I get sermons from *Time* magazine. They call me the 'current events' preacher." He brings credibility to his sermons on current issues because he has a long history of involvement in the civil rights movement, "and now I'm involved with the homeless and other issues." Dr. Joseph Lowery, president of the interdenominational Southern Christian Leadership Conference founded by Dr. Martin Luther King, is a personal friend of Moore's and has preached at United church on several occasions. Moore remembers that during the 1960s he took an Adventist Community Services van to a major march to provide medical care to the protesters, "and the union president called me in with my conference president and told us some of the White brethren thought we had lost our way." He did not back down, and today a new generation of young Black professionals is reaping some of the benefits their parents fought so hard to obtain.

Moore is enthusiastic about his people and the ministries they have developed. "We have a lot of younger professionals. People are more affluent today; they have better jobs. In fact, this congregation has the highest per capita giving in the conference. But they are still willing to witness!" One man leads the homeless ministry operated by the church, which includes emergency beds, transitional housing, and a Bible study group, as well as a street feeding program with teen and young adult volunteers. An elder is director of AIDS surveillance for the Georgia State Health Department, and he and other health professionals run a community health ministry that includes blood collections, nutrition classes, and health counseling. A deacon is chief of the homicide unit of the Atlanta Police Department, and has helped organize "Law Enforcement Appreciation Day" at the church. A U.S. Army chaplain who was baptized into the congregation from another denomination two years ago has developed a family life ministry, and is heard each week on local radio and television.

"We put a lot of emphasis on fellowship," comments Moore. There is a singles ministry, a senior citizens ministry, a youth ministry, a support group for women, and currently seven adult Sabbath school classes meet on Sabbath mornings and six small groups meet during the week. An active hostess and hospitality committee greets worshipers on the front steps, and ushers escort them to their seats. Many of the new members are newcomers to the area. "They move here from the Northeast to find jobs." Most are African Americans; perhaps 5 percent or less are West Indian immigrants.

Moore conducts a Revelation Seminar every year instead of traditional evangelism. He uses a classroom style—no music and a teaching presentation instead of preaching—four nights a week for eight weeks. He encourages the group to break in with their questions, and has not had any difficulty getting decisions. "I start talking about baptism right away, and once I've introduced the

Sabbath, I bring the seminar group into a special Sabbath school class. The Sabbath after the seminar graduation we schedule a baptism." Three lay Bible ministers help with visitation.

A Witness on Capitol Hill

Many Black churches are inner-city churches, but that does not necessarily mean that they are made up largely of poor people. The Capitol Hill Seventh-day Adventist Church in Washington, D.C., is attracting record numbers of Black baby boomers: young professionals. Senior pastor Wintley Phipps is a baby boomer himself and has developed a unique ministry to the rich and powerful. Although he is a Canadian, and not involved in politics, he is regularly invited to sing at such diverse but prominent events as Jesse Jackson's speech at the Democratic National Convention and Ronald Reagan's White House Prayer Breakfast. But when he went to the Capitol Hill church in 1985 it had only 155 members and was located in a row house. Three years later it had purchased and rennovated an historic church building and had 400 members, with an average Sabbath attendance of 600. The project received a real boost from an evangelistic campaign by W. C. Scales, Jr.

A pastor must understand the corporate personality of his church, believes Phipps. "Each church has a personality of its own. I soon realized I had inherited a church that was spiritually and emotionally demoralized, so I had through the grace of God to try to stir up some sense of confidence as well as self-worth and direction in the congregation." He told the congregation, "I think it's important that we keep an Adventist presence on Capitol Hill" just a few blocks from the seat of the United States national government. The church caught that vision and decided they should move into a new building but not far from Capitol Hill.

Members inviting their friends is the key to evangelism on Capitol Hill. "It's like the woman at the well running and telling everybody," says Phipps. "Every Sabbath morning we have about

100 to 150 visitors." He works hard to build fellowship during worship. "I think it is just a normal response to the presence of the Spirit of God. I think the sense of joy we feel in our service is and transmitted to those around us through love and hugs and prayers, and all during the week we find our people calling each other on the phone and praying with each other," sharing their needs and joys and becoming friends. "In the middle of our service we stop. First of all, we sing. Then we take time to have each member turn to the members and visitors around him or her and say, 'God loves you, and so do I.' People go to different parts of the building and give a hug and shake hands, so people immediately feel welcome."

Phipps wants worship to be Spirit-led and spontaneous. "We want to plan, but not too much," he says, "because sometimes if you're not careful, you can plan the life out of something. The church must be especially in tune with the Holy Spirit. It could be as simple as singing the chorus of a song one more time—because the Spirit has given you an impression that His people need that." At the same time, "the pastor himself, in terms of his message must be spiritually and intellectually prepared," preaching from careful study, not off the cuff. Phipps focuses his preaching on the spiritual and relational needs of his audiences. "Your messages have to reflect the specific needs of the congregation."

Of course, music is a very important part of worship at Capitol Hill. In fact, because of his status as a recording artist, some of his members are as eager to hear Phipps sing as they are to hear him preach. But he doesn't sing every Sabbath, and has encouraged a number of other talented young musicians to participate. The congregation sings some songs that are not in the hymnal, and may stop to memorize a new song from time to time. "Some churches try to incorporate fourteenth-century music" as the major style of worship music. "But," says Phipps, "I think it's a mistake, a generally misguided notion, that somehow fourteenth-century music is better than twentieth-century music. God wants us to be contemporary, to express ourselves in our context, as they did in theirs.

Contemporary spiritual music plays a great part in our worship."

Another Inner-city Church

Churches crowded with young middle-class Blacks are interesting because they break stereotypes; stereotypes of what Black churches are like and that middle-class churches cannot grow rapidly. At the same time, there are still hundreds of Black churches discipling large numbers of the poor. The gospel of Jesus Christ is still especially good news to the poor, and the "salvation and lift" factor still works. The Adventist Church, with its commitment to Christian education, has been especially successful at enabling low-income converts to teach values of self-discipline, hard work, and thrift to their children, who become teachers, technicians, managers, and professionals.

An excellent example of an Adventist church successfully ministering to the poor is the Ephesus church in Los Angeles. It began in May 1980, with 50 members. On December 31, 1989, it had 735 members. Craig Dossman, the founding pastor at 37 years of age, is still there after 10 years and "not going anywhere," and the church is still growing at 31 percent a year—the highest growth rate in the Pacific Union Conference in 1989. Ephesus church was spawned by the 54th Street church and met in a public park until a building could be found. "We don't have many middle-class members," says Dossman, but the congregation has managed to raise more than $400,000 to purchase and renovate a factory building, and to tear down five neighboring buildings in order to create 65 parking spaces.

Ephesus church has two worship services each Sabbath, and combined attendance averages 900. The 8:00 a.m. worship is focused on the needs of the very poor fresh off the streets. "The Lord's Table," a breakfast for the homeless, is served to about 150 each week at 9:00 a.m. (The homeless ministry also makes available showers, clothing, and a limited number of overnight beds.) Twenty Sabbath school classes meet at 9:45 a.m., and the second worship is at 11:00 a.m. Both worships are "very spirited

. . . celebration-style." Dossman says, "Our people come from many denominations, and they bring the richness of their backgrounds." He seeks to set a tone of acceptance and openness. "We don't care how people look and smell." There are at least 50 visitors every Sabbath, and "we will love them even if they never join the church."

Music is a very important part of worship at Ephesus. It is "very uplifting, upbeat . . . gospel songs, spirituals." There are three choirs and an orchestra. Prayer—serious emphasis on prayer—is also an essential element. "We need the Holy Spirit in our lives," Dossman says. Time is given to affirming praises for anniversaries, etc., and people are encouraged to voice their requests from the congregation. Lay ministers quietly go to stand with those who express a need, and then they are invited to come forward as one of the elders prays. And the leaders of the congregation meet every Sunday morning in a special prayer time to undergird the overall program of the church.

Dossman prefers to preach in series on topics like prayer, how to know God's will, the baptism of the Holy Spirit, the church and its mission, family life, singles, Christian living, as well as prophecy and the three angels' messages. He sometimes uses audiovisuals—a rear projection screen and slides. "I work from a yearly spiritual curriculum designed to meet the needs of the people." And he makes an altar call every Sabbath; first a call related to the theme of the day, and then calls to begin Bible studies and to join the church. As individuals come forward a team of lay Bible ministers is ready to stand with them, and then take them aside after worship to pray with them and get them started. "We average a dozen or so each Sabbath."

Most of his members are young adults, first generation Adventists, and poor people. And Dossman works hard to involve them in ministry. "We can celebrate on Sabbath because we are active during the week in the service of the Lord!" Ephesus church has 28 Home Bible Fellowships, and Monday nights are set aside for them. Each group is no larger than 15 and includes nonmembers as well as church members. These groups are scattered from Compton to Watts to Long Beach—all through central Los Angeles County. Dossman really believes in small group evangelism. "In Acts 2, I found that there were two types of meetings in the early church. Not only did they gather regularly at the temple, but they also met daily in their homes to break bread and to have fellowship. I had been stressing only a Temple ministry . . . no house ministry. There was something lacking." He also says that he discovered the importance of delegation and building up lay leaders. He has visited Paul Yonggi Cho in Korea, and is writing a Doctor of Ministry dissertation on the subject at Claremont Theology School. "We baptized 177 people in 1989 from the ministry of these laymen," he says. "I baptized about 80 as a result of public evangelism."

Church members also conduct Daniel seminars and Revelation seminars, and staff an astonishing array of social ministries—drug and alcohol counseling, a homeless shelter, New Dawn Women's Center, a "story hour" van that reaches out to latchkey children and gang kids, a "church on wheels" ministry on Skid Row that distributes at least 350 meals every Sabbath afternoon, a family life ministry with marriage seminars and workshops on how to get out of debt, cooking schools and weight-control programs, a singles ministry, a youth ministry, a women's ministry, activities that get men in the church together with boys who have single moms, and a prison ministry because "we are located in the 77th Precinct, which is the highest crime area on the West Coast," smiles Dossman. "I work as an enabler; an inspirational coach." Every Sunday morning at 8:30 he prays with his elders and key leaders and spends time in planning. "Wednesday nights are for training." Dossman has an associate pastor and a Bible worker, and they are also involved in supporting lay ministries.

He has had conflict "about the cultural orientation of some members toward worship . . . about my preaching and the style of music . . . about the focus on the homeless." The conflict built up and came to a head in early 1988 when Dossman had two major surgeries and had to take off three months to recuperate. Several of the original families who helped found the new congregation pulled out and transferred to other nearby Adventist churches. "The Lord showed me I was doing too much, and I told the Lord, 'If You get me out of here alive, I will train and encourage the people.' In the past three years, we've taken in 450 new members."

Without footnoting specific quotes and facts, in addition to personal knowledge and a number of interviews, I have used information from the following:

Azure Hills Seventh-day Adventist Church bulletin and inserts, Dec. 6, 1988.

Daily, Steve. "Church Growth Bloweth Where It Listeth." *Spectrum,* vol. 19, No. 3.

Dossman, Craig A. "Operation Reach Out." Unpublished manuscript.

Eva, Willmore. "Wintley Phipps, of Capitol Hill." *Praxis,* Fall 1988, pp. 4, 6.

Graybill, Ron. "Church Growth in Black and White." *Columbia Union Visitor,* Sept. 1, 1985, p. 2.

Halstead, Linda. "Celebration Center Holds First Services." *Pacific Union Recorder,* June 5, 1989, pp. 8, 9.

Hawley, Don. *Set Free!* 155120 S.E. 122nd Ave., Clackamas, Ore.: Better Living Publishers, 1989, pp. 67-78.

Jacobsen, Don. "A President's Viewpoint on Milwaukie." *Administry,* Summer 1988, p. 11.

Jensen, L. Paul. "Campus Ministry in Orange County." *Meeting the Secular Mind: Some Adventist Perspectives.* Berrien Springs, Mich.: Andrews University Press, 1987, pp. 168-175.

Milwaukie Seventh-day Adventist Church bulletin, August 19, 1989.

Simpson, Dan. "Azure Hills—Where Church Is Exciting!" *Administry,* Summer 1988, pp. 14, 15.

Snyder, David. "The Milwaukie Experience," *Administry,* Summer 1988, pp. 9, 10.

Versteeg, Norman. "The Church of the 1980s Must Have Correct Priorities." Unpublished paper read at the First Theological Consultation, Glacier View, Colorado, August 1980.

———"Twelve Years in One Church." *Ministry,* April 1981, pp. 14, 15.

CHAPTER 7
Can It Happen Anywhere Else?

THE MILWAUKIE, Azure Hills, and Garden Grove churches are all West Coast congregations. Members of White Adventist churches in the rest of North America are generally viewed as more conservative. Congregations in the Midwest and Northeast are decidedly smaller, and the Adventist presence is considerably less than in Oregon and California. Can the same thing happen in a less favorable environment? Can it happen in the East? Can it happen in the small church? Can anything be learned from these stories that can be replicated in your local church?

In fact, about 30 percent of the 4,500 local congregations in the North American Division are showing some growth. And 10 percent are growing at a rate in excess of the division-wide average, although most of these congregations are ethnic churches that are drawing their new members largely from recent immigrants to the United States and Canada. Nonetheless there are stories of significant growth among smaller White Adventist churches located away from the West Coast.

The Suburban Adventist Church is the only White church in Buffalo, New York, a metropolitan area of 1.2 million on Lake Erie with two Black Adventist churches and one Hispanic church. It has a new building, but it is located some distance from the central city, "at the beginning of a county road three miles from the nearest bus stop." This is a "rustbelt" town with a significant annual out-migration of residents and church members, and few people moving into the area. It is an ethnic, blue-collar city where more than half the population is Roman Catholic. The population has well-established social and religious bonds, "so there is not a significant group of people open to new friendships, new religious ideas, or a new church home."

When Eoin Giller arrived as the new pastor in 1984, attendance was down to 70 or 80 each Sabbath. "There had been no prayer meetings or social events for a considerable period of time. . . . Young marrieds, young people in general, were in the minority," and there was considerable conflict. By 1986 attendance was averaging 174 on Sabbath mornings and 85 at midweek meetings. This is an annualized growth rate of about 66 percent. "Members, and especially young people, are bringing their non-Christian friends to church," Giller reported. "We usually have eight or more regular visitors and five to 10 new visitors each week."

Giller faced conflict, as did his brothers on the West Coast. "Group goals in Buffalo seemed to relate more to internal Adventist concerns . . . than to reaching out to bring people to Christ and the church." The members looked on a scheduled evangelistic crusade as "imposed by the conference," and even though the evangelist was Kenneth Cox, one of the best in North America, "we were unable to assimilate the majority of the converts because our own people had not been prepared to socialize with new members."

"I realized that it would be a fatal mistake to cross the established power group in the congregation, so while seeking to draw other factions into the decision-making process, I worked with the group in control. This procedure made it more difficult to conduct an efficient board meeting because we had to spend as much time in maintaining a positive emotional climate as we spent in getting through the agenda."

Giller came prepared for a ministry of revitalization. In 1977 he had completed a Doctor of Ministry at Andrews University with a project that involved church renewal in a small, rural congregation near the seminary. At the beginning of that project the congregation had 50 members with 32 in regular attendance. A year later it had 54 members with 45 in regular attendance; a growth rate of 8 percent in membership and 41 percent in attendance. In the project Giller perfected a step-by-step process for change, using a consultant role, which he would use again as senior pastor at Buffalo Suburban church.

He described the renewal process in a 1986 *Ministry* article. "The first step in church revitalization is to analyze. One must ask, 'What is going on in both the community and the church?' The second step . . . is to accomplish an effective 'entry' to the church." The third step is to build relationships in the congregation and "bring new life to the worship service." The fourth step is to introduce the church to a planning process and help them set clear goals. And the fifth step is to "enlist the laity in ministry."

Worship at Buffalo Suburban church includes Christ-centered sermons and an open, listening attitude. "We moved a large screen and the overhead projector onto the right side of the platform, and introduced songs of praise," remembers Giller. "New music has brought new life to us." One of his members says, "The songs of worship and praise lift my spirit and allow me to forget my troubles and listen to the sermons. I get hope at church now!"

A youth orchestra with two dozen brass and wind instruments complements the organ. The choir sings contemporary Christian music as well as the old favorites. "We brought our lay activities service into the church service as 'Ministry Matters,' locating it after" the praise time, says Giller. "I interview people . . . and affirm members for service to the church. . . . I preach sermon series . . . all practical. . . . They develop the feeling that we are on a spiritual journey together. And the gospel of saving grace allows me to make frequent altar calls to which new folk respond easily. People do not leave the sanctuary saying, 'So what!' "

"We ceased to use the bulletin as a ritual for worship." His goal was "to develop a liturgy that had at least one element that

would minister to the needs of each person. Worshipers need to feel
the presence of God . . . regardless of their age, social background,
or religious sophistication. . . . Ritualistic formalism promotes unbelief and the death of the missionary spirit in a church." The
service begins at 10:45 a.m. and ends at 12:15 p.m. The sense of participation is enhanced by the young people in the orchestra because
it is rare to see young people leading out in worship, and by the
practice of inviting a different church member to assist the presiding
elder on the platform each Sabbath.

Small groups were also introduced to the Buffalo Suburban
church. The Friday night practice sessions of the orchestra include
Bible study and fellowship time. When Giller restarted the prayer
meeting on Wednesday nights, he placed the chairs in a circle in a
carpeted upper room and introduced praise songs and life application Bible study such as a series on how to stay on top when things
get tough. He says, "Now on Wednesday evenings people of all
ages gather at church for supper. Men and women come directly
from work. . . . We conduct a 'Tots for Jesus' class and . . . a
Pathfinder Club. So we do something for every member of the
family. . . . We usually see new faces each week. . . . New people
are thus introduced to the church on a regular 'church night' rather
than on Saturday—for most, a strange day to worship."

Giller has used friendship evangelism as the primary strategy
for finding new members. He has found that conducting classes on
how to give Bible studies "usually does not effectively help
members to reach out into the community. . . . We rely on teaching
members how to invite others to Wednesday night meetings, to the
church and to seminars. . . . This year only eight people came to our
Revelation Seminar in response to the thousands of fliers we sent
out, but 28 came because of friends in the church. . . . We have a
regular 'Friend Day' when members . . . invite nonmembers to
attend church and return home for lunch with them. People now feel
secure enough about the church, the quality of worship and content
of the sermon, to invite friends to come any given Sabbath. In fact,
some of the people who most enthusiastically invite their friends to

attend are not yet members of the church." Each Sabbath every newcomer is given a welcome packet with information about Suburban church, its community services, ministry, and beliefs. Atlantic Union Conference president Philip Follett says this "became one of the most significant elements" in the congregation's outreach. He describes Friend Day as a "dynamic event that challenges every member to bring at least one nonmember friend on a special Sabbath. This nudges members into introducing their nonmember acquaintances to the church's program, and became a significant entry event for the church." The church also has a tape ministry and a weekly radiobroadcast.

"The pastor's intimacy with his members plays an especially important role in preparing the church for growth," Giller believes. "If the pastor is distant, the church will take his model—and visitors will sense a distance between themselves and the members." "I had been taught at college to stay outside the various social systems of the church. However, study in a clinical pastoral education program convinced me that the pastor and his family can be friends with his people." The key to this relational process is the monthly elders meeting at Suburban church. "Here our worship structures are monitored, attendance and church growth are discussed, and various problem areas are assigned to someone to manage. Consensus building and a 'player-coach' approach to shared ministry is linked to prayer and a love for our church." Innovation has taken place in many areas of church life, and Giller has discovered that it is "important to use informal consultation with members and introduce change for a trial period—to be reviewed at the quarterly business meetings."

Another example of how significant church growth can happen, even in the Northeastern region of North America, is the Stamford, Connecticut, Adventist Church. Lower Fairfield County has 500,000 residents, but only a handful of Adventists. They commuted more than 30 miles to neighboring metropolitan areas and had unsuccessfully tried for years to start a congregation or even a branch Sabbath school. This is an upper middle-class bedroom community for the second-largest complex of Fortune 500 company headquarters in the nation—a very hard-to-reach target group. In 1978 Tony Moore was asked by the Southern New England Conference to plant a church in this area. "Not understanding the demographic impossibilities," he smiles, "we accepted the challenge." He started with a small group of 12 members, and by the time the congregation was officially organized in January 1980, about 40 adults were in regular attendance. Today membership is 104.

"Sabbath morning . . . is the single greatest evangelistic opportunity of the church," asserts Moore. "Services must be positive, practical, and filled with praise to Jesus." People also need fellowship. Many of the residents of Stamford are transplants from distant cities. "They had no family," says Moore, so "we opened our home, often having up to 80 people for Sabbath dinner. Then we would take the people for a walk at the nature reserve and close the Sabbath together. This was repeated year in and year out. The wonderful thing was that people who came the first year and were discipled began to disciple others the next year. Soon there were several families inviting others to their homes or picnics for fellowship and Bible study." A midweek Bible class and home visitation program are also part of the strategy.

Moore stayed 10 years with the Stamford church. He reflects that "after our early success one year into the program, I was ready to go and hold evangelistic meetings in other areas. Dr. Charles Stokes counseled me to stay there and make the work solid. This was excellent but distasteful counsel. It was much more appealing to ride the wave of evangelistic excitement. We decided to stay on and repeat the program each year for the next several years." The important step of obtaining a physical plant for the new congregation was also taken slowly. In 1981, three years into the project, "a two-and-one-half-acre property on a major road, in the finest section of town," was purchased. Five years later a funding and construction plan was presented to the conference committee. An 8,500-square-foot building was completed in 1987, "eight years after we arrived in Stamford." Long-range planning and step-by-step follow-through seem to be key factors to the success of this new congregation.

Even in the unreached communities of the urban Northeast and in churches like Buffalo Suburban who have passed their centennial anniversary, significant growth is possible.

In all parts of North America there are similar stories waiting to be told. The Arlington church, near Fort Worth, Texas, has grown from 300 to 500 members in two years. "A third of this growth has been through baptisms, another third through transfers, and the other third has been added by reclaiming and establishing inactive Adventists," says senior pastor Jim Gilley. It is a congregation that attracts and ministers to single adults and young couples. "An effort is made to create a loving, nonjudgmental atmosphere in which all can grow in grace." The 11:00 hour is called "Saturday Morning" and features "positive messages on finding true happiness, overcoming such problems as fear, worry, guilt, and stress."

The Roseville church near downtown Sacramento, California, had plateaued at about 175 members for decades. Between 1987 and 1989, it added 200 new members and has an average worship attendance of about 400, with the leadership of Pastor Ron Clouzet. Inactives have been decreased from 34 percent of the membership in 1987 to only 13 percent in 1989. The annual growth rate in membership is above 50 percent. The key factors again are emphasis placed on prayer and the gifts of the Holy Spirit, a dynamic worship service, a strong sense of belonging among the members, rapid incorporation of new members, visibility in the community, and a boldness for outreach. "We have gone from being 100 lazy Adventists to a group that takes its mission very seriously," comments one of the lay leaders.

What About the Small Church?

Nearly two out of three Adventist churches in the United States and Canada have 100 members or less, and any discussion of church growth or innovation is usually met with the objection that "it can't be done by the small churches; it doesn't fit their needs." Small groups are especially resisted because "we are already a small group." It may be a case of identifying chicken and egg. Do small churches stay small because they have not found a way to grow or are they small because they have resisted growth over the years? A key element in breaking the barrier of 50 in average Sabbath attendance is becoming a "multicell" congregation with more than one fellowship circle.

Even small churches can have spectacular growth. In the late 1970s I pastored a congregation in Charleroi, Pennsylvania, a blue-collar mining and steel mill town south of Pittsburgh. Deindustrialization had just begun, and unemployment was very high. Many younger families were moving to jobs in the Sunbelt. With its roots in East European ethnic backgrounds, the community is dominated by the Orthodox and Roman Catholic churches. Yet the 40-member congregation had a vision for outreach and a heart to love people. In the two years that I was there it grew to more than 50 members— an annual growth rate above 10 percent—and Sabbath attendance increased from 30 to more than 60.

When I introduced the small group concept, the lay leaders were enthusiastic and immediately started four family home groups as a replacement for prayer meeting at the church. The first quarter, two of the dozen nonmembers participating in the groups made decisions for baptism, and several groups have continued to operate each year since that time. My first experiment with the Friendship Evangelism Seminar was in that congregation, and soon several members were bringing their neighbors and relatives to Christ. Small churches can grow, and the tools for growth are the same as for large churches.

Another example of how growth can turn around even the most difficult situation can be found in the Hillsboro, Ohio, Adventist Church. Located in a small town of 5,600 in rural Highland County (population 32,000), membership dwindled to 27 in July of 1985. Six lived out of state, 10 had not attended even once in two years, and another had dropped out more recently. The active members included three couples and a single woman between 30 and 65 years of age, and two women in their 80s. Sabbath attendance averaged seven. There had been no baptisms for five years.

The congregation was in grave crisis because in 10 years it had made no headway in paying off the mortgage on its building. The union conference revolving fund could no longer extend or refinance the loan, and the local conference was in no position to write off the obligation. A local Protestant group indicated it would like to purchase the facility, and the Adventist members were discouraged. Pastor Jose Osorio had two other churches and was completing doctoral studies at Andrews University, so he had comparatively little time to invest in the Hillsboro church.

But within three years the congregation tripled its regular Sabbath attendance and boosted its membership to 38 while trimming a number of inactive and out-of-town names on the roster. Osorio introduced the small group concept to his four lay leaders and they began to invite relatives, neighbors, and friends to home Bible studies. He also planned special Sabbath morning series designed to reach out to nonmembers. He encouraged the congregation to share their musical abilities, instead of sticking to traditional singing from the hymnal. Slowly at first, new life and growth came back into the group, and amazingly they met their mortgage payments and covered the cost of outreach materials and audiovisual equipment! Small churches can grow, and the approach is just as relational as it is in large congregations even when it is tailored to rural small town culture.

What Are the Transferable Concepts?

Innovation and church renewal is happening in North America. There is risk in these changes, but there is also risk in refusing to change. As Steve Daily has observed, "the fastest growing, most youthful congregations in Adventism believe they are led by God's Spirit to break out of the old wineskins of formalism and to worship

God in dynamic, contemporary forms." What can we learn from these case studies in church growth? What are the recurring themes in each story? Six basics seem to be fundamentally important.

1. A pastor with strong relational skills who is able to build a team of lay leaders and infuse the congregation with a sense of mission. These pastors are not necessarily quotable theologians, excellent writers, or highly skilled administrators. In fact, they seem very ordinary men in their 40s and 50s until you watch them interact with leaders, members, and visitors. They embody an active, unsentimental love with a strongly spiritual tone. They are open and able to listen, but unambiguous about the direction and future of their ministry. They are willing to leave the details of complex programs in the hands of others, but they can reach across the mountain of specifics and understand how to touch the lives of harried, hurting men and women.

2. An inclusive, supportive, and happy fellowship. These congregations are made up of very average middle-class, suburban people—many of them baby boomers who have somehow discovered they can enjoy religious activities and find daily, practical meaning in their faith. They have somehow let go of the personal reserve and "privacy" concerns so typical of middle-class North Americans, and opened up to the possibility of regularly making new friends and sharing their inner joys and sorrows with these friends. They feel the presence of the Holy Spirit in their fellowship and have a sense of freedom to be accepting toward people who are different, and forgiving toward people who make mistakes. They actively care for one another in times of crisis and transition, and readily speak about the spiritual meaning attached to these events, and the resulting needs felt by the people who experience them. They aren't afraid to pray and ask for God's presence with them as they struggle and bear one another's burdens.

Newcomers are quickly made to feel comfortable, and everyone is encouraged to think of the church family as a "safe place" where they do not have to pretend to be in control, on top of things, or even successful Christians.

3. A more participatory, kinesthetic, and personal style of worship than the liturgy to which conventional Adventism has become accustomed. As Southeastern California Conference president Steve Gifford correctly observes, this kind of worship is not remarkable in Black churches. In fact, it is the norm. It is new to White Adventists and disturbing both to those who see church as a dutiful routine and those who define "reverence" essentially in terms of silence, not rapture.

The preachers in these growing churches put more emphasis on "Christ-centered and practical messages" than they do on "truth-filled, straight testimony," not because they shy away from preaching Adventist doctrine, but because they know that if the cold abstractions of doctrine are not made to touch the life situations of their hearers with warmth and compassion, the good news will not be heard or adopted.

There is nothing different about their theology. They are not on a crusade to reform the fundamental teachings of the church. They simply realize, perhaps intuitively more than conceptually, that modern man is lost among the mass of information, the countless logics, and the competing claims of so many, many belief systems. That what he, and she, wants more than anything else is just to "come home," find Someone to trust, and not attempt to sort it all out and arrive at finely tuned ultimate answers. To put it in terms perhaps understandable only in my own generation, it is the picture, not the pixels, that touches our hearts.

These preachers have learned to communicate with the "TV generation" to lead worship that can be experienced as well as observed. They want their congregations to know the presence of the Holy Spirit.

4. Christian music in the contemporary idiom. The importance of music in the worship and life of these growing congregations cannot be underestimated. Musical gifts that are solidly grounded in Christ, and in touch with current popular forms, are essential to a growing church today. The hymnody that developed

400 years ago in the Reformation has always been at odds with movements for evangelization of the masses. Early Adventists sang gospel songs to well-known, secular tunes. Today there is a plentiful supply of new Christian music composed specifically for singing praises to the Lord, and in order to reach out to the unchurched, it partakes of the acceptable elements in popular music. Those who label it "rock" or "jazz" display their ignorance of contemporary culture, as well as their prejudice. No congregation can expand if it uses only a narrow range of music. No individual member should expect to like everything that is presented. That is not the point! The point is to reach out and share the good news of a living God with people in deep need. It is important to use music skillfully, to plan it thoughtfully, no matter its vintage—to carefully weave a musical pattern that brings individuals of diverse tastes and experiences together before the Lord, caught up in the urge to praise Him. That takes a very skillful, widely read musician with pastoral insight and theological understanding. A competent minister of music is almost as important as a visionary senior pastor. Your local church does not need to use the same music that is used at Buffalo Suburban or Milwaukie, but it must find a range of music that expresses the joy of serving the Lord and brings contemporary people, including the unchurched, into an attitude of praise.

   5. An active, ongoing strategy of small groups. The highly visible Sabbath mornings in these congregations is really only the tip of the iceberg. The essential infrastructure is made up of "cells" in the body of Christ—choirs, Bible study groups, Sabbath school classes, working groups, Home Bible Fellowships, orchestras, support groups, seminars, etc. As much pastoral focus and energy is devoted to nurturing groups as to caring for individuals. The leadership team clearly understands that small groups constitute the framework on which the whole congregation stands or fails, so they work hard at starting a constant supply of new groups, meeting diverse needs, and getting everyone into a group. A mark of the importance of the small group strategy is when the office of elder or "lay pastor" is synonymous with group leader.

6. Targeted, permanent ministries instead of events, activities, and short-term programs. These congregations have discovered that in today's world ministry does not happen on schedule. They have found that you cannot plan three weeks, or even six weeks, once a year for evangelism that really touches the lives of the unreached. Nor can you plan a special Sabbath once a year to really nurture church members with special needs. The secret of making disciples for Christ in our contemporary culture is to build consistent, ongoing relationships with many segments of the community. A rally, a 10-week seminar, any activity by itself, cannot be real outreach. It will just never bridge the gap between the world of the churched and the multiple worlds of the unchurched. Events are just tools. It is the consistency of a team of people who are present with the target audience year in and year out, regularly demonstrating their compassion and reliably meeting needs, that wins a hearing for the gospel in today's secular, urbanized society.

Most traditional church activities were invented in an age when Protestant, small town America had a seamless culture. Market segmentation has shattered that culture. The high-tech society generates a need for "high-touch" ministries, and random, short-term activities are not "high-touch" in character. The fabric of an ongoing ministry is essential to the success of any particular seminar or event. That is why these churches work so hard to build ministries with permanent teams, staff support, weekly small group meetings, monthly large group meetings, newsletters, marketable names, and expanding networks of volunteers and participants.

Are these six points doables or dreams? Of course, they are doables. That is where I began chapter 6; looking at certain fast-growing congregations to see what they do. Can they be replicated? They are being replicated every day in scores, hundreds of local churches. The next several chapters will take a more detailed look at some of the how-tos. But it is important to remember that one of the key elements is the unique, home-grown nature of all successful congregations.

Information about transferable concepts is valuable to any creative leader, but the wooden implementation of recipes will get you nowhere. The Spirit cannot bless when some pastor or congregation "cooks out of a book." Only when you dream and experiment and struggle under His leadership will you find the way.

Without footnoting specific quotes and facts, I have used, in addition to personal knowledge and a number of interviews, information from the following sources:

Giller, Eoin. "Building Up the Body of Christ: A Study in Church Revitalization Leading to Church Growth." Doctor of Ministry dissertation, Andrews University, 1977.

————"New Life in the Church." *Ministry*, December 1986, pp. 16b-16e.

Gilley, James. "A Growing Church." *North American Division Ministerial Association Bulletin*, Spring 1988, p. 25.

Moore, Tony. "The Stamford Story: Anatomy of a Faith Venture." *Praxis*, Spring 1989, pp. 9, 11.

"Roseville Church Shows Dramatic Growth." *Pacific Union Recorder*, Oct. 2, 1989, p. 20.

CHAPTER 8
Small Groups:
The Next Wave

I N THE early 1980s a new kind of public evangelistic meetings emerged among Adventists in North America—the "seminar" approach. It did not replace, but certainly eclipsed, the conventional "crusade." Harry Robinson is generally credited with inventing the new method, while pastoring in the Texas Conference, and certainly his Revelation Seminar has become the most popular form of seminar. He describes the differences between the new approach and the conventional public meetings. "Teaching, rather than preaching, techniques are utilized. . . . There are no program features or preliminaries (e.g., no song service or special music)." And seminars are conducted largely by local pastors and church members, not professional evangelists.

Although in some ways seminar evangelism still partakes of the era of institutional evangelism, it is also the first step into the era of relational evangelism. Robinson says, for example, "it is largely materials-centered" as opposed to being "personality-centered." But he also says, "The teaching mode is a two-way communication between speaker and audience. The preaching mode can be better characterized as a one-way communication." And he asserts that another "outstanding characteristic of the teaching mode is the use of homework assignments . . . completed in preparation for the next topic, which he contrasts with what he calls the "surprise system" in "traditional preaching."[1]

Mark Finley, while an evangelist in the Southern New England Conference and director of the NAD Evangelism Institute in Chicago, together with Russ Potter, president of Concerned Communications, developed the "sequenced seminars" strategy in which a cycle of seminars is begun with topics of a nonreligious nature related to the felt needs of nonmembers and then moves logically and step by step toward doctrinal study. This is an even more relational approach than the basic Revelation Seminar. It has been developed in a number of forms more recently, especially with the creation of evangelistic family life seminars.[2]

By 1987 a Columbia Union Conference study stated that seminars "continue to be the most popular form of evangelism" with attendance ranging from 7 to more than 150, and noted that more laypersons were conducting them. It admitted that "seminars produce fewer baptisms for each person attending on opening night than traditional evangelism, even though a greater percentage may stay." And it reported that all of the pastors interviewed "agreed that the key to baptisms was having attenders get to know church members. But many also expressed difficulty in getting members to mix with nonmembers in useful ways." So the pastors said they visited the nonmembers in attendance, and were able to baptize those with whom they built a relationship. They lamented the lack of personal ministry skills on the part of most of their lay leaders.[3]

This report mentions Revelation seminars held in a home, and even as early as the 1986 article by Harry Robinson, a sidebar prepared by one of the *Ministry* editors states "the most recent development from Texas is a 'Home Series' version designed for use by laypersons conducting seminars in homes rather than in a public meeting hall."

In fact, by the end of the 1980s the largest number of Revelation seminars were being conducted in homes. Pastors had learned that the relational element was the key to success. This is clearly revealed in a set of suggestions from pastors published in the Spring 1989 issue of *Praxis*.[4] "We close the evangelistic series with a banquet," says Carlton Cox, a pastor in Philadelphia. "We want everyone to know that to be one with us has loving and appreciative benefits. It is a must that prayer and study groups continue throughout the year." Marty Thurber, a pastor in the New Jersey Conference, which has had one of the best growth rates in the East, stated, "Our churches have grown because of warm fellowship, Sabbath-evening activities for young married couples, Friday night vespers, and studies and socials. . . . People are motivated by friendship." Paul Barcemas, pastor of a four-church district in Minnesota, said, "Our most successful means of evangelism has been Revelation seminars conducted in various homes."

Small Group Evangelism

Early evidence of the emergence of small group evangelism can be seen in the 1981 church growth study conducted by the Institute of Church Ministry. Small groups had a high correlation with church growth in the survey of pastors. "A high percentage of the membership meeting in small fellowship or study groups is the second strongest predictor of actual growth" in local Adventist churches across North America the study concluded, and a further examination of the data reveals that this is especially true in White English-language congregations. The survey of members of White churches ranked small groups among the five most important predictors of church growth. One church member in four reported that he or she was participating regularly in a small group.[5] By 1989 small groups were the single most widespread method of soul winning in North America, as reported in the annual survey of programs and activities conducted by the NAD.[6]

Perhaps the most significant breakthrough in small group evangelism came in 1988 when the Oregon Conference launched its "Homes of Hope" campaign. In 1987 it had conducted 228 Revelation seminars, all beginning in March with coordinated advertising and promotion. This led to an ambitious goal. A total of 2,000 small groups would be planned, "opening a home of hope in every neighborhood" in the conference, and new "relational Bible study" materials would be produced for these small groups. Two major rallies were conducted to introduce the concept. A Sabbath of fasting and prayer was set aside, because "unless the Homes of Hope neighborhood Bible study ministry is bathed in prayer, it will be just another program," said conference president Don Jacobsen. More than 1,000 church members were trained to lead groups at 10 training events in January. A total of $100,000 was used to print the materials and undertake an advertising campaign that included direct mail to every home in the state, personal invitations delivered by members to their friends and neighbors, and a yard sign marking each location. A total of 800 groups actually got started in February. The groups met weekly for about 20 weeks, and then interested nonmembers were invited to join the pastor's Bible class at the nearest Adventist church.

Non-Adventist attendance averaged two or three per group. Results varied greatly from place to place. "Some groups had no nonmembers attend initially," said Garrie Williams, Oregon Conference ministerial secretary and project coordinator. Other groups began "with up to 12 nonmembers, and even after one or two weeks were looking at the necessity of dividing. In some areas groups [were] multiplying rapidly." Grants Pass, where Skip Bell had introduced small group ministries in the early 1980s, had 50 home Bible study groups. A small congregation in Cathlamet, Washington, had four groups with 16 nonmembers in attendance. Other small churches found that this approach worked well. Veneta had seven groups with a total attendance of 53, including 26 nonmembers. Junction City had two groups with 11 nonmembers. Beaverton church reported that more than 100 people attended on the first night of its groups.

By mid-1989 about 700 people had been baptized from small group evangelism. A total of 1,239 neighborhood home Bible study fellowships had functioned during the 1988 "Homes of Hope" campaign, and another 500 were held in the first half of

1989. Of the 1988 groups, 820 used the original materials on the book of Revelation, 381 used a second set of materials on the Gospel of John, and 38 used other materials. And the concept had begun to spread rapidly. At least 736 small groups functioned outside the Oregon Conference in 1988 and 1989 using its materials—422 in the North American Division and 276 overseas. In fact, by mid-1989 so many requests were coming to the Oregon Conference staff for presentations at conference workers' meetings that they decided to take a "you come to us" approach, and set up a weekend for those from across the NAD who wanted to come and see what was happening. More than 250 pastors and conference staff showed up for this meeting, and another one is scheduled in 1990.

Some have felt that the materials developed by the Oregon Conference are not really "relational Bible study" in nature. Even Williams, one of the authors, describes them at times as "inductive" in approach. "We could call it the discovery method," he says, contrasting it with "the didactic method" used in the Revelation Seminar materials. He outlines three steps used in the Oregon study guides. "First, the person is led to discover what is in the Scripture. . . . The second part is where the person begins to interpret the text. . . . The third step is that the person, on the basis of his discovery, makes a decision." The examples that he gives stress the importance of leading group members to apply the Bible in their own life situations. Precise definitions are probably not as important, as the fact that for the first time Adventist Bible lessons take into consideration the small group dynamics that will convey their message to individuals.

The relational dimension was clearly in the thinking of Oregon Conference leaders when they designed the "Homes of Hope" strategy. "The concept grew out of a need that was expressed by . . . church members and pastors," reports Kurt Johnson, Oregon Conference church ministries director. "After almost 1,000 members and pastors had conducted and assisted with Revelation seminars in homes, churches, and public buildings, two observations were expressed. First, the seminars held in the homes were more relaxed and personal, which allowed for close relationships to be formed very quickly" and created an open atmosphere in which fewer nonmembers dropped out. Second, "the close relationships gave them the support to encourage continued attendance when difficult doctrinal issues were discussed. . . . It is better to go slower and longer in the instruction period and maintain the students by developing true friendships."[7]

One significant finding of the 1988 "Homes of Hope" project distinctly defines the relational nature of what is going on in Oregon. "Where churches were relying wholly upon the handbills to bring people to their groups, this has been a disappointment," says Williams. "The handbill will, in some areas, draw people to respond who would never otherwise be contacted, but in most places the handbill is a backup for the personal invitation." It is "a friendly contact with neighbors and work associates" that brings the "greater possibility of success." Johnson states simply, "very few people respond to a handbill for a home study group." In fact, the Oregon Conference leaders came to believe that even if they had not spent considerable sums on direct mail advertising, the total attendance would have been about the same.

Although it may not work everywhere, Oregon's emphasis on small group evangelism has been highly successful for a number of its local churches. The Springfield church near Eugene has in two and a half years increased its Sabbath attendance by 80 percent and in 1988 it had the largest number of baptisms in any White congregation in the conference. It sponsors 30 small groups, each led by a lay pastor. At the 300-member Gresham church in a suburb of Portland, attendance was steadily declining when Don James became pastor in 1987. A combination of small groups, Sabbath celebration, and lay pastor training has, with the power of the Holy Spirit, doubled Sabbath attendance in 18 months. At least 45 of the 120 local churches in the Oregon Conference are continuing to maintain a program after the "Homes of Hope" campaign was completed. Small group evangelism does generate significant church growth. "Virtually every church that is growing today, in the Adventist Church and elsewhere," says Williams, "is doing so on the basis of small groups. As we trace the history of Christianity, we see from the beginning that small groups have been the dynamic factor in the growth of the church."

The Background of the Small Group Concept

In fact, small group evangelism is not a new idea. The early church as it is described in Acts and the Epistles had as its primary form the house church, not the congregational assembly that we are so accustomed to. (See Acts 2:44-47; 4:32-35; I Cor. 16:19; Rom. 16:5; Philemon 2.) The essential Bible terms used to describe the church are body, bride, household, and vineyard. Each carries the basic idea of the church as the community of God's people, a people called to a special task or "vocation," (see Eph. 4:1). They become "church" when the dimension of fellowship or *koinonia* is added. The principal characteristic of the New Testament church is its intense, interactive common life. Christ chose 12 men and formed a small group as the basis of His ministry on earth. He stated that His purpose in asking the twelve to be His disciples was so they could "be with" Him and He could "send them out," (Mark 3:13, 14, NIV). The most important point that Christ makes in His "priestly" prayer is that there must be a quality of life together among Christians that exhibits to nonbelievers a deep love, a tough love that knits the body of Christ in a manner similar to the unity of the triune God, (see John 17:20-23). If the remnant church at the dawn of the twenty-first century is to really impact the world, it must do so through high-quality instances of *koinonia* that are positioned at the points where the purposes of God meet the needs of mankind. Real ministry can happen only through groups of people who are seriously attempting an inward journey of faithfulness and fellowship and an outward journey of service and evangelization.

In Adventist tradition, small group evangelism has been called "cottage meetings." Ellen White was familiar with the Wesleyan "class meeting" because of her upbringing in the Methodist Church. She repeatedly urged the Adventist Church to take this approach seriously. "The formation of small companies as a basis of Christian effort has been presented to me by One who cannot err," she wrote in 1902. "Let the members be formed into small companies, to work not only for the church members, but for unbelievers."[8] Again in 1909, she writes, "In the home circle, at your neighbor's fireside, . . . in a quiet way you may read the Scriptures and speak a word for Jesus and the truth."[9]

As early as 1871 she had written a simple, practical piece on how to conduct meetings that demonstrates her grasp of the Methodist "class meeting" and includes a clear understanding of small group process still valuable more than a century later. "Meetings for conference and prayer should not be made tedious . . . Formality and cold stiffness should be laid aside. . . . What is the object of assembling together? . . . We meet together to edify one another by a mutual interchange of thoughts and feelings, thus making one another acquainted with our aspirations, our hopes, and gathering strength, and light, and courage from one another. . . . From the light which I have received, our meetings should be spiritual and social. . . . Reserve, pride, vanity, and fear of man should be left at home. Little differences and prejudices should not be taken with us to these meetings. Like a united family, simplicity, meekness, mutual confidence, and love should exist in the hearts of brethren and sisters who meet to be refreshed and invigorated by bringing their lights together. . . . All have not the same experience and the same exercises in their religious life. But those of diverse experiences come together, and with simplicity and humbleness of mind, talk out their experience. . . . of daily trials, conflicts, and temptations, strong efforts and victories, and great peace and joy gained through Jesus. A simple relation of such experiences gives light, strength, and knowledge that will aid others in their advancement in the divine life."[10]

This passage obviously undercuts those who state that Ellen

White would not approve the sharing of inner feelings that often occurs in small groups, and those who think that only an abstract, unemotional style is appropriate in Bible study. It puts the lie to those who state that small group evangelism is based on "secular humanism and psychology." It is ironic that after all these years, as Williams reports in Oregon, "some older lay leaders have been a little uncomfortable with the relational type of Bible study.

"It is new to Adventists and not all can adapt easily to it. Some have said they prefer the 'fill in the blank' type of study guide. It is important that the leaders work with what they are comfortable with. However, it must be remembered that in many areas the 'fill in the blank' type of study has proved rather ineffective in the end. People become not thinkers but the reflectors of other persons' thoughts, and this does not help in making strong decisions."

As urbanization has created an anonymous mass society, and mobility has separated most North Americans from their childhood friends, and changes in family life have caused more loneliness, it becomes more and more essential to bring people to know Christ's plan for their lives in the context of a supportive, friendly group. Interdenominational church researcher Lyle Schaller says that in congregations of more than 350 members, almost all new members come into active fellowship through small groups. Any congregation that has one or more small groups has potential to grow simply because it has "doors" through which new people can find entrance into its social fabric. Another researcher from a small, conservative Protestant denomination—Dr. Flavil Yeakley—observes that in growing churches the adult Sunday school has smaller class sizes and small groups, but in declining churches he finds larger, lecture-oriented classes.

"The churches that are growing the fastest are more likely than stagnant or declining congregations to have a strong small group program in place," reports the Barna Group, an independent, evangelical market research company in Glendale, California, based on numerous surveys of churches across the U.S. "Small groups represent a viable means of introducing people to biblical concepts in a less threatening, low-key environment." The Barna polls give evidence that about 8 percent of the unchurched population in the U.S. is participating in Christian small groups—a total audience of 10 to 12 million nonbelievers being evangelized. "The people involved in small groups operated through the church were much more likely to consider the sponsoring church to be 'their church.' Thus, by providing a meaningful opportunity to grow as a person and as a Christian, the individuals strengthened their allegiance to the local church itself. . . . Many participants have experienced a significant change in lifestyle and attitude." The Barna Group studies found that "the vast majority of small groups use the Bible as their primary text . . . the most common schedule calls for weekly meetings . . . usually somewhere between 75 and 120 minutes per session." Key activities included study, fellowship, prayer, and community outreach.

Some Adventists oppose small groups simply because they are so widely used in some other denominations now. Even in Ellen White's day the borrowing of methodology from other faiths seems to have been an issue. "I have been shown that in our labor for the enlightenment of the people in the large cities, the work has not been as well organized or the methods of labor as efficient as in other churches that have not the great light we regard as so essential," she wrote in 1892. Then she appealed for more training for Adventist workers and less "preaching." In 1909 she pointed out that "the work of bringing the message of present truth before the people is becoming more and more difficult," and appealed that "it is essential that new and varied talents unite in the intelligent labor for the people."[11] Think how she might evaluate the degree of difficulty faced by Adventist evangelization today, and then you may be able to comprehend what kinds of "new and varied" ministries she might recommend.

Why is a small group strategy so crucial to church growth and the evangelization of North America today? Organizations work better when they are designed around groups rather than individuals, observes Harold Leavitt, professor of organizational development at Stanford University. Small groups satisfy human needs, "providing a range of activities for the individual members, support in times of stress and crisis, and settings in which people can learn to be reasonably trusting and helpful to one another." Groups also "are good problem-solving tools, useful in promoting innovation and creativity. They make better decisions than individuals do." They are "great tools for implementation, gaining commitment from members so that group decisions are likely to be carried out willingly." Small groups help to "fend off many negative aspects of size, preventing communication lines from getting too long, the hierarchy from getting too steep, and the individual from getting lost in the crowd."[12]

All of these issues are present in the current struggle of the Adventist Church for renewal and growth. The Adventist Church in North America has had tremendous growth, jumping from a small community of 250,000 in 1950 to what will be a major denomination of 1 million by 2000. It is finding it difficult to digest the fruit of that growth. How can we satisfy the greater range of human needs coming into the church; the diverse, pluralistic interests, attitudes and cultures of so many different kinds of people? How can we maintain the participatory sense of ownership and involvement on the part of so many people? How can we overcome the inappropriate level of individualism that was present among the much smaller and scattered flock of the first half of this century? How can we keep the necessarily larger and more complex organizational structure from getting so tall and steep that it crushes the front lines where growth actually is generated? The small group approach can keep the momentum of the Advent Movement alive in the 1990s and beyond. Our mission and message will not thrive in the Northern Hemisphere unless it adopts a small group strategy.

A Support System for Ministry

Most Adventist church members will not maintain concentrated and effective ministry to the unchurched unless they have the support of a small group. Perhaps one of the best ways to understand the role of the small group in the total life of the congregation is to see it as a support system for lay ministry. There are many different formats for group life, ways to define the "right size" of group, and terminology used among the hundreds of current, practical books and articles that have been published to describe how to do small group ministry. There are some generalities that are common to all packages and systems, and essential to any successful small group ministry.

Group Size: There are really two basic sizes of group work. The "small group" is anywhere from three to 12 people. It is most effective at 8 to 10 members. The "mid-sized group" is 15 to 40 people. It can be conducted as a seminar or class, or the "workshop" technique can be used in which an up-front leader conducts the overall meeting, but breaks up the group into smaller clusters of four, six, or eight for certain assignments. No one has discovered why, but some personalities are more comfortable in small groups and some are more comfortable in the mid-sized groups. A strong church program will include opportunities for both.

Sharing: In order to break the ice and bond with the others, each individual in a group needs time to talk about what is happening in his life, to share his feelings and tell his story. This is how group members get to know one another and come to trust each other. This sets the atmosphere for the entire session and future group meetings. Effective processes are needed to allow people to share at a pace and level they are comfortable with. People want to know and be known to each other, but they do not want to move to topics that are too personal too soon.

The primary technique that is used is to start each session with one or two questions that are easy and even fun to answer, and go around the circle getting a short answer from each person present. Many of these icebreakers have been published, and leaders can easily be taught to write their own "sharing questions" if the materials they are using do not include them.

Once a group has been together a few times, it is normal for there to be one or two individuals who take a greater share of the time at each session to concentrate on some need or crisis in their lives. As long as the spotlight is rotated somewhat equally among the group members from session to session, this works well, allowing the group to minister to the most needy in its circle without being overcome with too much pain or too many details to remember. When one person in the group continually takes the time of the group, this can be damaging or even destroy the group. Skilled group leaders learn to gently restrict the behavior of those prone to make themselves the center of attention.

Study: Serious study of the Scriptures is central in all groups. But the approach taken to Bible study will be quite different depending on the needs of the group members, their religious background, level of education, and preferred style of learning and group participation. A wide range of Bible study techniques and materials have been developed. Roberta Hestenes, who was for many years professor of Christian nurture and education at Fuller Theological Seminary, has cataloged more than 20 approaches to group Bible study.[13]

Developed by Stephen Haskell in the 1880s, the question and answer method has served the Adventist Church well, but it has come to focus on abstract propositions, and as used in recent years lacks emphasis on the application of Scripture to the life of the reader. Also, among people with greater education there is great interest in studying the Scripture in context instead of just key texts organized around principles, themes, or doctrines. This has given rise to methods such as inductive, discovery, and relational Bible study.

Discovery Bible study is a method in which questions guide a person into seeing and understanding the key points being made in a portion of Scripture or a major theme that runs through many Scriptures. It focuses on the Bible, but also on what can be learned from the Bible. It is an approach perhaps halfway between the classic question-and-answer method used in older Adventist Bible lessons and the inductive method. The adult Sabbath School quarterlies currently use an approach like this.

An inductive Bible study focuses on the Scripture itself and what can be learned from it without regard to a larger system of doctrine. A portion of Scripture is read, then three questions are asked: What does this tell me about God? What does this tell me about myself? What does this tell me about what I need to do? Its greatest strength is that participants learn to dig in the Bible and appropriate its riches for themselves, instead of having it neatly packaged up and served to them by others.

A relational Bible study focuses on the student and how he or she relates to the Bible message, and on what it teaches about his relationships with others. The technique is simple. A story from the Bible is read. Then each group member is asked to think of himself or herself as a participant in the story. This may be done through preassigned journaling, quiet time to paraphrase the Scripture passage in writing, or simple meditation for a few seconds. It can be done with a direct question. For example, How would you feel if you were Peter and had just denied your Lord? Second, group members are asked to tell which of the characters in the story they identify with and why. The third question is What is the good news for me in this story and why? Although relational Bible study is too subjective to form a basis for establishing doctrines, its great strength is that it brings the emotions of the participant into contact with Scripture and allows everyone, no matter his lack of prior Bible knowledge or turn of mind, to get involved.

Basic to all three methods is the application of Bible teachings in the secular life of the believer. How do I apply this in my life? With my spouse and family? On my job? In my neighborhood and civic duties? The Adventist message can be adequately taught through any of these methods. Its truth is not dependent on any particular approach, just as it does not require any particular translation of the Scriptures to prove Adventist doctrines. Various approaches may speak of the Adventist message in different terms, but the faith and practice of those brought to a knowledge of the truth through these varied methods will in all essentials be the same. Adventist publishers are beginning to make available study materials of all three major types. For example, the Sabbath school teaching helps published each month in *Celebration*.

Support: The New Testament commands that believers should bear one another's burdens (see Gal. 6:2). This is most commonly done in small groups by simply praying for each other. A key element in nurturing and caring for each member is to ensure that at each group session members have opportunity to share the joys and burdens on their hearts, and to hear someone pray for them. Some small groups are known simply as "prayer groups" because they spend most of their time and energy on this and have a relatively undeveloped approach to Bible study. In any case, a strong prayer life is essential to the success of a group's ministry.

But real support often requires more than prayer, as Michael Slater, pastor of Temple Baptist Church in LaHabra, California, points out in his book *Stretcherbearers*. He quotes Proverbs 18:24, "There are friends who pretend to be friends, but there is a friend who sticks closer than a brother." Then he asks, Whose name would you put in this text as your "friend who sticks closer than a brother" or sister? Who could you call at 3:00 in the morning if you were in real need? And he asks, Would anyone put your name in his Bible in this text? He points out how superficial fellowship can become in the typical, middle-class church in North America. Unfortunately Adventist churches are not much different.

Referring to the story in Mark 2 in which a sick man is let down through the roof, Slater points out that we do not have to have *the* answer to the problems of another person—an all-inclusive, comprehensive solution. We are simply called to do what we can under the circumstances. He teaches his congregation to pray for imagination and faith in meeting the needs of others. "Give of yourself," he says and urges each member to do more than say "I'll pray for you."

"Sometimes you're on the stretcher and sometimes you carry it," Slater says. It is always a team effort—no one can carry a stretcher by himself. "Stretcher times" happen when least expected; we all go through them; and they are destructive when no one knows how to care for the hurting. "It's a lost ministry," declares Slater. "No one knows how to do it anymore. If we get the church doing it again, it will result in church growth." He quotes a gang kid explaining why he joined: "When you're cared for, you'll do about anything."

The task of helping has become so specialized and governed by such a bureaucratic system that the average church member simply doesn't know what to do to be useful in a time of crisis. "My friend is hurting but I don't know what to do, so I don't do anything." An increasing number of small groups are using a prayer request technique that Slater developed. A written list is made of specific needs that looks like this:

NAME	MAIN ISSUE	SECONDARY ISSUE
Jones	marriage falling apart	Counseling—collection to pay Volunteer baby-sitting Two guys take him out Tuesday Women take her out Wednesday Get card to deliver money, etc.
Smith	unemployed	Help her make a résumé I'll type it 4 people volunteer to pray for her and call her each day

The group or congregation is asked to concentrate on simple doables related to the smaller, secondary issues while praying about the major issues. They also pray for the success of the specific action steps. This is done once a month, not every session. Every successful small group must find some way to provide practical help to its members when they are in need. Of course, the specific help and how it is organized will differ according to the kinds of personalities, background, and needs present in each group.

Service: The Barna Group surveys indicate that among the common problems in small group ministries is the formation of cliques. Groups can turn inward to the degree that they become self-centered, a "holy huddle." New persons can no longer feel at home in the group—it is "saturated" and unable to evangelize. This seems to be a particular problem in Adventist congregations where many pastors who have attempted to start small group outreach report that the groups proved to be useful only for "nurture." Interdenominational church growth expert Carl George says that Adventists have "koinonitis"—inflamed fellowship—because we are so busy talking to ourselves we have forgotten how to talk to outsiders. This tendency is ultimately destructive of the church's mission.

A simple way to guard against this self-centered tendency in groups is to insist that each small group have some service project to those outside its circle. This may simply be an "empty chair" that the group prays about and seeks to fill from among their own unchurched acquaintances. It may be a more elaborate ministry within the congregation, or in the community. The healthiest and most effective small groups are those that target a particular group of unchurched persons whom they work to reach and bring to Christ and fellowship in the church. This approach is discussed at length in the next chapter. It may begin with a commitment to study material that is primarily suited for the needs of the nonmembers who will be invited instead of choosing material primarily of interest to long-established church members.

Leadership: Small group ministry will fail unless it is led by lay volunteers. A general rule in growing congregations with successful small group strategies is that none of the groups are led by the pastor. The Barna Group surveys indicate that there is uneven quality in group leadership and a lack of willing lay leaders. What pastors must address is the recruitment and training of small group leaders. Sometimes this is linked with the office of elder. It is biblical to expect that elders will be undershepherds, each with a small flock of his or her own. Other churches find that the largely ceremonial and administrative duties of elders have become traditional in the congregation, and that it is impossible to change these expectations. They often create a new role of "lay pastor" with appropriate training and duties—essentially leading and caring for a small group, including the prospective members attracted to it and its ministry to the community.

The key method by which a pastor enables his or her elders or lay pastors to function as effective ministers is a regular meeting of an inner circle in which the expectations for the leadership of the small groups are modeled. A simple rule for growth is that no one gets to sit with the pastor or gets his primary attention unless that person is leading or launching a group. The pastor becomes a disciple-maker rather than a caseworker. This council of elders or church ministries council should include leaders of ministries and key programs and committees as well as conventional Home Bible Fellowships and study groups, but its agenda should always focus on the ministry these units have with people, not the administrative details.

A useful evaluative technique is to go through the entire membership list from A to Z, and ask which group, committee, or program is ministering to each individual or household. Several observations will come to light: (1) a list of people to whom no cell in the body of Christ is ministering, many of whom are inactive; (2) a list of families "cut up" between several different ministries; (3) a short list of individuals involved in so many activities that burnout may be a danger; and (4) distinct "parish clusters" related to each small group, Sabbath school class, and program or fellowship unit. The smallest churches will have only a single cluster. This information can easily lead to planning for a strengthened and growing church.

Getting Started: Initiating a small group strategy is not achieved successfully by taking the church membership list, dividing it into groups of a dozen, and assigning each to an elder. Many churches have tried this approach and consistently have failed. Groups must be voluntary. Their participants must choose to join. Leaders must have some special gifts and preparation. The leaders and participants must learn to think and act in new and different ways than most congregations have traditionally been accustomed to behaving. All of this takes time, intentional progress, and considerable prayer.

It is best to begin by setting an example. The pastor might invite a consultant from the conference staff, an experienced lay leader, or a neighboring Adventist pastor to lead a group for six or eight weeks. He may do it himself. Selected church members are asked to participate so they can see what it is all about. At the end of the series, participants are challenged to consider being trained to lead a group themselves.

The next series of about 10 or 12 weeks would be devoted to conducting a leadership training group. This would include three aspects, as well as the basic features of any small group ministry. Leadership of the individual sessions would be rotated among the group members, giving each an opportunity to lead on at least one occasion. Some time would be spent in a study of the principles and skills of small group ministry. Time would also be devoted to planning for the groups that the participants will launch. Curriculum resources for this kind of training group have been published.[14]

Then three, four, five, or more groups would be started throughout the congregation and community, each led by one or two of the participants in the training group. These groups might run for 6 to 12 weeks as an initial "covenant period" before a general retreat is held to evaluate the congregation's move into small group ministry and to plan for its further development. At this retreat the pastor, key lay leaders, participants in the original two groups and the leaders, and at least one representative from among the participants of each of the small groups that have been started should be present. They would come together to share what they have learned and assess the results; to celebrate the presence of the Holy Spirit and the work of God in their congregation; and to establish bold plans for future growth based on a careful view of the needs in the congregation and community. This plan would be the charter for a small group evangelism strategy in that congregation, owned by the lay leadership and strong enough to move the church ahead for several years.

Small Groups Versus Established Programs

The introduction of a new approach always creates a certain amount of defensiveness and uncertainty among those who are well schooled in the long established methods. Does a shift to small group evangelism do away with the seminar approach or conventional public evangelism? How do small groups relate to Sabbath school classes and midweek meetings? Are small groups as good as they are said to be by their advocates, or are they a way to move into a "holy huddle" and avoid the hard work of evangelizing a secular, urbanized North America?

A major objection to a small group strategy for church growth on the part of some has been the fact that many of the small groups started by certain highly visible pastors in the 1960s and 1970s were largely nurture-oriented. Small groups, like any other form of ministry, can be outreach or nurture, or both. It depends on the goals and work of the leaders. If they are positioned as outreach vehicles from their introduction, and leaders are carefully selected and trained with an evangelistic purpose in view, then small groups will be tools of evangelization, not self-centered ingrownness.

It is important to understand that small group ministries do not do away with the need for public evangelism. Garrie Williams points out that in the Oregon Conference "Homes of Hope" experiment, the "reaping" happened in "50 evangelistic crusades," which "averaged 15 baptisms." Some large, fast-growing churches may not hold traditional crusades, but their Sabbath morning attendance has a high percentage of unchurched people in attendance, and the pastor's Bible class functions as a constant "reaping" mechanism. Many people, because of their personality and cultural preferences, are brought to a decision and incorporated into the church at the one-to-one or small group level, but many others, because of their personality and religious background, need the opportunity to hear the gospel preached in a larger assembly and the challenge to take a stand in a public way. The 1990s will be a decade of both/and, not either/or.

The Sabbath school should not be seen as being at odds with a small group approach. It is the traditional place in Adventist practice where small groups have continued. Through decades of evolutionary change, the typical class has become less and less effective as a small group, but it did not start out to move in that direction. A key place for small group evangelism to happen is on Sabbath morning in the Sabbath school. It will require the willingness to introduce new classes of a different style alongside the conventional Sabbath school. These "branch Sabbath schools on the premises" should be designed to reach out to audiences that do not find the conventional program appealing, particularly the unchurched. They should be given a full 90 minutes to function in their own space. Some should be small groups, while others should be medium-sized seminar groups, and still others workshop-style classes in which a leader directs the group in both seminar and breakout group time. Maximum evangelistic potential is achieved in the Sabbath school when a "menu" of possibilities is offered.[15]

Small groups can be seen as the death or the salvation of the midweek meeting. By the early 1980s less than a quarter of Adventist churches in the NAD still had a weekly prayer meeting. Less than 10 percent of the members attended where prayer meeting continued. By introducing a praise service, fellowship around a light supper, a variety of choices, or replacing prayer meeting with highly publicized seminars of various kinds, some churches have been able to revitalize the midweek meeting. But these have usually been short-lived experiments or transitional structures that eventu-

ally brought the church to replacement of the midweek meeting
with a number of small groups meeting at different times and
locations during the week. Even in small churches with less than
50 members, the introduction of two or more small groups instead
of one Wednesday night meeting has always resulted in significant
increases in total attendance. More options simply allow more
people to participate.

What Kind of Small Group Works Best?

More and more I am being asked at meetings and in phone calls
and letters to point out "the best type of small group program."
Some people think I am being flippant when I respond, "The kind
that works best for you." The essential nature of the small group
approach is its flexibility. It is so crucial to church growth in the
1990s because of the increasingly segmented and pluralistic world
we face. There is no one answer to be applied across the board to
all congregations, or even a primary answer to be given to "average" churches. Many different approaches work very well in many
different situations. Current research needs to focus on finding the
factors involved in the best "fit" between situation and kind of
strategy.

The Redlands church uses a form of small group evangelism
called Home Bible Fellowships (HBFs), as do many other churches
in California. HBFs are formed each fall and spring, and their study
is coordinated with the Bible passages from which the pastor is
preaching on Sabbath morning. "It is best . . . to speak on the theme
chapter at the close of the week in which the HBFs study that
chapter," says Phil Jones, senior pastor. The groups "are formed
according to common interests and common life passages, not
geography." Elders play a key role as conveners and facilitators of
the HBFs. "The typical HBF meeting lasts one and one-half hours
with social mixing time for the first 20 minutes, Bible study for one
hour, and 10 minutes for prayer request time. Each person
covenants to pray daily for the other members. Evangelism is

accomplished by using the 'empty chair' method during the closing prayer. . . . An empty chair is drawn into the circle and prayer is offered asking God to send someone next week to fill this chair to whom we can minister His love." This congregation has experienced growth from HBFs, as have the others that use it. The Harvest 90 Adventist Research Taskforce (HART) is working on the further development of this type of small group evangelism.

Several Hispanic churches in California have had considerable success with a small group strategy like that of Paul Yonggi Cho in Seoul, Korea. Church members are assigned to groups organized on the basis of geography. The groups meet weekly, and each church member in attendance is assigned a job description. "For example," says Pastor Miquel Cerna, of the Norwalk Spanish church, "director, assistant, secretary, treasurer, personal ministries director, telephone secretary, deacon, light bearer, Sabbath school representative, youth representative, etc." Each group is assigned a missionary territory to work weekly and is expected to "hold its own evangelistic meetings each year." Each group has a written plan for outreach, and elders are assigned "as supervisors of a number of group leaders." Cerna says he expects "regular reports from the leaders and elders" and holds "training seminars regularly to challenge and inspire leaders and elders." While pastoring the 40-year-old Hispanic congregation in the Van Nuys suburb of Los Angeles, he "saw 350 new members baptized in just two years of small group ministry. At the end of 1984 the Norwalk Spanish church had 70 adult members. In 1985 those members saw 71 added to their membership through small group ministry. . . . In 1986 the same church had 140 baptisms as a result of their small group ministry."

This approach is highly structured, but still very relational. Cerna insists that his group leaders "allow time for each member to share the joys and trials of the week," and says, "we train our leaders to speak no more than 20 percent of the time. . . . The leader acts as the facilitator." Every member is involved in the evangelistic purpose of the small groups. There are objectives for outreach, and "each individual sets his or her own goal for Bible studies and for baptisms." "We devote 10 to 15 minutes at every meeting to analyzing the evangelistic activities of the group." This includes "developing a 'rescue plan' for any member who was absent from church the previous Sabbath."[16] This is the same kind of small group strategy that has been taught for several years by Sam Monnier, an associate director of church ministries at the General Conference, in his Maranatha Lay Evangelism Training Seminars (LETS). It has been used quite successfully by Anglo churches in New Jersey, Indiana, and Pennsylvania.

A quite different type of small group ministry has sprung up in the large cities in the Northeast. In 1982 Samia Chway-Chway, a young Lebanese Adventist who works at the World Bank headquarters in Washington, D.C., began a lunch-hour group on Thursdays. Bill Liversidge, a church growth consultant who was then on the staff of the Columbia Union Conference, helped her get it started with a four-week seminar on identifying personality styles and understanding how to work with them. Rob Randall, while pastor of the suburban Silver Spring church, later led the Bible study. It grew to a regular attendance of 20, and then a second group was started on Wednesdays with Pastor Ron Halvorsen, then pastor of the Takoma Park church. The bank management insisted that the groups "must be strictly nondenominational, that no distinctive doctrines of any church shall be emphasized," so the leaders have focused on leading people to Christ. Private Bible studies have resulted, and people have been baptized. Total attendance at the two groups is now about 50 each week, and a layperson—Baxter Fanwar—leads both groups. Employees come in from other agencies in the same building and across the street: "the International Monetary Fund . . . the American Red Cross, George Washington University, and the Federal Deposit Insurance Corporation."[17] A similar group has been organized at the American Electric Power building in Columbus, Ohio. Several small groups in the San Francisco metropolitan area have formed a network called the Bay

Area Young Adult Fellowship (BAYAF). It includes more than 450 young Adventists, many of them no longer attending church, who work in the highrise offices, laboratories, and shops. This approach holds much promise for reaching the large cities and should be duplicated in hundreds, if not thousands, of downtown locations across the United States and Canada.

Another small group strategy is to focus on the particular needs of specific kinds of life situations. This is called the "support group" concept. Sometimes this begins among a particular segment of a congregation. For example, in January 1989 six Adventist military families currently stationed at Scott Air Force Base in Illinois formed a "military support group." The group has a prayer chain, and helps each other deal with common problems unique to military families, as well as planning to "spearhead an outreach program in the military community and an inreach program in the church to educate others about SDAs in the military." One of the first things the group did "was to cut and deliver a load of firewood to one of the local church members [as] a way to say 'thank-you' to one of the church's matriarchs, and a way to become integrated into and more involved with the local SDA church."[18] Singles ministries often begin as small support groups. The support group concept can also be used in follow-up work with unchurched people who have attended stop smoking clinics, stress seminars, weight control programs, etc. While pastor of the Allentown, Pennsylvania, church, I baptized people from the "Strugglers Group," which was made up primarily of graduates from the extensive health education outreach sponsored by the church.

The changing role of women in North American society may be threatening to some Adventists, but it can also be an opportunity for small group evangelism. Women's support groups have been organizing by the tens of thousands for two decades, but one of the first Adventist churches to see them as a vehicle for evangelization is the Corona church near Riverside, California. The GLOW ministry began in 1986 with the leadership of associate pastor

Sharon Hanson and lay coordinator Jean Hermann. Every Wednesday women's support groups meet at 9:00 a.m. and 7:00 p.m. in the church. The morning group begins with a continental breakfast and the evening group with fruit juice or hot drinks. The sessions begin with aerobics, praise, prayer, and music. There is a get-acquainted time and a Bible study. Then the group breaks out into "elective classes," including a newcomers' class for first-time attenders and options on topics such as child rearing, working women, crafts, parenting teens, self-esteem, marriage, divorce, and weight control. Child care is provided with games, songs, stories, and a snack. GLOW is advertised in the community as "a weekly get-together especially for women . . . a warm, friendly atmosphere . . . an opportunity to make lasting friendships [and] . . . an interdenominational study of God's Word." Special events for the entire family are planned about once a month. Direct mail has been used and has brought in a number of new participants, but, says Hanson, "to be honest, the most effective way to get new GLOW members has been friends bringing friends." Attendance runs 50 to 100 a week, and Hanson is kept busy with pastoral visits and Bible studies that result from the support group. A similar ministry began the same year at the Battle Creek, Michigan, church. It is called the Mother's Center and is described in the appendix to *The Making of a Mother* by Karen Spruill (Hagerstown, Md.: Review and Herald Pub. Assn., 1988).

Another very practical approach to small group ministry puts emphasis on the already existing fellowship circles and working units in a congregation. Can the committees, the choir, the Pathfinder Club staff, the Home and School Association, and other groups become "Christian communities" in which spiritual support and personal sharing, Bible study and nurture happen as well as the handling of organizational tasks? Particularly for older members with a more traditional view of the church and what they expect from it, a committee can be as good as a Home Bible Fellowship, if it includes prayer and Bible study, personal sharing and involvement in outreach. For example, a choir leader who sees that the fellowship and ministry of the members is as important as the quality of the music, and who includes a time of Bible study and sharing in "choir practice" will find that the choir becomes an avenue for outreach and nurture alongside its music ministry.

The genius and the essence of the small group approach is that there is no one way to do it. It is flexible, creative, and multifaceted. It can be reinvented in each situation. It calls, as does the New Testament, for church members to bring a praise, a lesson, a revelation, or an interpretation when you come together, for the edification of one another (see 1 Cor. 14:26). It is personal, intimate, and relational; it is spiritual, Bible-centered. It allows for the fine-tuning to thousands of vastly different needs, communities, lifestyles, and personalities that is necessary for the continued evangelization of North America's complex society in the 1990s. It is the next wave; the technological breakthrough for God's church in today's world.

---

1. Harry Robinson, "Revelation Seminars: Making Them Work," *Ministry*, December 1986, pp. 18-22.

2. Donald A. Eckenroth, Jr., "The Development and Implementation of a Sequential Evangelistic Program in the Local Church," unpublished Master of Arts thesis completed at Andrews University School of Graduate Studies, May 1984.

3. Kermit Netteburg, *Revelation Seminars: What's Happening in 1987* (Columbia, Md.: Columbia Union Conference Communication Department, 1987).

4. A journal on pastoral practice published by the Mid-America and Columbia union conferences of the Seventh-day Adventist Church.

5. R. Dudley and D. Cummings, *Factors Relating to Church Growth*, p. 22, Table 30; pp. 64-69, Tables 31-33; and p. 47.

6. Monte Sahlin et al., "Survey of Lay Leaders: Activities and Programs in 1989," North American Division Church Information System Report 2, January 1990.

7. Kurt Johnson, *Successful Small Group Evangelism Guide* (Clackamas, Ore.: Oregon Conference, 1988), p. 1.

8. E. G. White, *Testimonies*, vol. 7, pp. 21, 22.

9. *Ibid, Testimonies,* vol. 9, p. 129.

10. In *Review and Herald*, May 30, 1871.

11. Both quotes are reproduced in the compilation entitled *Medical Ministry* (Mountain View, Calif.: Pacific Press Pub. Assn., 1963), pp. 300, 301.

12. *Behavior Today*, Dec. 2, 1974, p. 317.

13. Roberta Hestenes, *Studying the Bible in Groups* (Philadelphia: Westminster Press, 1983).

14. Two Adventist curricula have been published: Clarence Schilt, *Group Builders Handbook* (Loma Linda, Calif.: Loma Linda University church, 1987); Skip Bell, *Together in Christ* (Mount Vernon, Ohio: Ohio Adventist Book Center, 1985). I also recommend Richard Peace, *Small Group Evangelism* (Downers Grove, Ill.: InterVarsity Press, 1985).

15. The new Sabbath school teacher training modules jointly produced by the North American Division and the Pacific Union Conference Church Ministries Departments include videos and workbooks that show how to develop an evangelistic Sabbath school using the approach described here. They can be obtained through local conference Church Ministries Departments and the NAD Distribution Center at Union College in Lincoln, Nebraska.

16. Miquel A. Cerna, "How I Use Small Groups in Evangelism," *Ministry*, October 1987, pp. 17-19.

17. Aurora G. Arceo, "World Bank Hosts Bible Classes," *Adventist Review*, Aug. 17, 1989, p. 22.

18. Jeanne F. Brooks, "Local Military Support Group," *For God and Country*, Second Quarter 1989, p. 3.

CHAPTER 9
Building
Effective Ministries

G ROWING CHURCHES in the 1990s and beyond will sponsor targeted, permanent ministries instead of events, activities, and short-term programs. Evangelism that is scheduled for three weeks or six weeks once or twice a year cannot really touch the lives of the unchurched. The secret of making disciples for Christ in our contemporary culture is to build consistent, ongoing relationships with specific segments of the community. A rally, a 10-week seminar, any activity by itself, cannot be real outreach. Events are just tools. It is the consistent ministry of a team of people who are present with the target audience year in and year out, who regularly demonstrate their compassion and reliably meet needs, that wins a hearing for the gospel in today's secular, urbanized society.

An example of this kind of ministry is the work of Joe Jerus and Paul Jensen, who have been conducting a campus ministry in the Orange County suburbs of Los Angeles since 1971. They have touched the lives of thousands of students and seen hundreds turn to Christ. They get in touch with people through opinion surveys and information tables set up in public areas on the campuses, and by sponsoring public speakers at campus events. "But," says Jensen, "our most effective method is through the friendships of people already involved in our ministry." They organize a large group activity each quarter to which students in their network can invite non-Christian acquaintances. "Last fall 125 attended a luau, and 80 came to host a Christmas party for the residents of the Orange County juvenile hall.... We usually give a short explanation of who we are and a 10- to 15-minute presentation relating the gospel to the theme of the evening," along with a question-and-answer time. Individual invitations are made to interested students to join one of the small groups offered by the ministry. "Presently there are eight groups, with a total of 80 to 90 people involved." Four couples form the core group that staffs the ministry. "The average time from our first meeting with a non-Christian through his or her becoming a Christian, individual growth, involvement in home Bible fellowship, congregational involvement, and finally membership is one to one and a half years."[1]

As I pointed out in a previous chapter, most traditional church activities were invented in an age when Protestant small-town America had a seamless culture. With urbanization and a more secular society, we now have a plurality of lifestyles in North America. Business calls it "market segmentation." National leaders refer to "pluralism." The many choices open to people today—the tendency to move often, cut ties with the extended family, live in large, anonymous metropolitan areas, and have a large number of short-term relationships—has shattered the traditional church culture.

At the same time, this high-tech society generates a need for "high touch" experiences. Unchurched people turn to the church and have a readiness to consider spiritual things at points of pain and times of transition in their lives. This requires "high touch" ministries—wholistic, long-term, and highly personal approaches, not random, short-term religious activities. These ministries are focused on people, on building relationships with people—not programs (although obviously they must include the activities that they do). The fabric of an ongoing ministry is the essential backdrop in the success of any particular seminar or event. That is why churches that are having some success in reaching out to the unchurched and discipling baby boomers work so hard to build ministries with permanent teams, staff support, weekly small group meetings, monthly large group meetings, newsletters, marketable names, and expanding networks of volunteers and participants.

Relational needs are the bridge to the unchurched. Touch points for sharing faith with the average American or Canadian who has little interest in organized religion per se include major life events such as moving to a new community, getting married or divorced, the death of a loved one, a career change, major illness or hospitalization, unemployment, and the birth of a child. Michael Coyner's research indicates that any unchurched person with a significant level of stress is likely to seek out a church or a source of spiritual care—a chaplain, a prayer meeting, a small group, a seminar, a counseling center, etc.[2] This has been validated in several studies among Adventist converts. There is an especially strong linkage between moving to a new community and joining the Adventist Church. "This research shows that mobile segments are producing tremendous growth for the church," reports Kermit Netteburg, director of the North American Division marketing program. "This should not be surprising, since people who move to a new area are willing to make all kinds of changes—including a change in religion. In fact, people who relocate are likely to be searching for ways to make contacts and settle into their new surroundings, and a friendly church group is an attractive means of establishing themselves." Local churches should reach out to newcomers in the community, he recommends.[3]

Family life concerns are one of the major reasons that unchurched young adults begin to shop around for a church home, according to recent studies by the Princeton Religious Research Center and the Glenmary Research Center. Other studies also indicate that churches meeting the needs of single parents and couples with young children will reap impressive increases in membership. During the 1990s, 30 million parents will have their first child and start searching for a church. Will we be prepared for the potential harvest?

Single adults, especially the recently divorced and widowed, search for a support network, healing, and new ways to find meaning in their lives. A million people are divorced or widowed each year in North America. Half of all marriages end in divorce. Are we prepared for this potential harvest? These are the focal points for evangelization of North America in the 1990s and beyond. "People need the Lord," asserts the contemporary gospel song, and they do! By the millions every day! Do we have ministries that can touch them? "The fields all are ripening," says the old hymn. "Where are the reapers?"

Many congregations feel the need to develop singles ministries, young adult ministries, women's ministries, prison ministries, family life ministries, deaf ministries, campus ministries, ministries to the poor, to businesspeople and opinion leaders, to children and parents, to recovering alcoholics, etc. Some have discovered how "target group" ministries can be fruitful evangelization—but often their attempts to do so are less than satisfactory. A clear view of the difficulties becomes quickly apparent. Where to get qualified people? How to develop something that has substance and continuity; that will have integrity among the general public? "We don't want people to feel that our ministry is a gimmick."

Observing successful ministries in a number of churches and working with scores of Adventist congregations as a consultant lead me to believe that the key to building effective ministries in the local church is careful, step-by-step development: a definition of the needs, adequate targeting and planning, quality communication with the target audience, a small team of church members who are willing to learn Friendship Evangelism skills, and a keen sense of how this ministry relates to a total church strategy of relational evangelism. With these five items in hand, any congregation can succeed in creating specialized "touch" ministries—Marriage Encounter, campus ministries, homeless ministries, prison ministries, prayer breakfasts for businessmen, women's ministries, Community Services centers, preschools, etc. These are the fundamental building blocks for relational ministries, so I have discussed them here at some length.

Defining the Needs

The way to begin a ministry is to "find a need and fill it," says Robert Schuller of the Crystal Cathedral. Of course the pastor, some interested church members, or the church board have a general sense of the needs, or they would not be seeking to get something started. But this general sense of urgency is not enough. Successful ministries "scratch where people itch." You need to know where your people—your congregation and your community—"itch" right now. How many are interested in parenting skills? in grief recovery? in finding a job? in dealing with divorce? in improving their marriages? How many are singles? How many are students? How many are prisoners or homeless or handicapped? What kinds of activities would be helpful to them? What are they willing to invest in time, money, and personal involvement?

One way to define needs is simply to assemble the statistical data already available. You can construct a family profile of your congregation by going through the church membership list and using the worksheets in the *Family Ministries Planbook*.[4] (If you are not acquainted with everyone in the congregation, have someone else go through the score sheet with you. Large congregations may need to do a survey.) The census data on file at the public library will quickly give you similar information about the local community—the number of teenagers, married couples, single parents, divorced persons, widows, or families with children under age 13, students, prisoners, low-income households, unemployed people, and various ethnic minority groups, etc. More highly defined demographics are available from the Institute of Church Ministries at Andrews University, Berrien Springs, Mich.

Statistical data will reveal the raw number of potential participants in various kinds of ministry, but cannot indicate their degree of interest or their "felt needs." Various survey instruments that can be used to find the interests of the congregation and the community are available. A simple questionnaire like those in the *Family Ministries Planbook* can be distributed to active members during a worship service. You will have to interview inactive church members and the general public by telephone or doorstep visits.

If you want to obtain even more specific information about the kinds of activities, topics, publicity, and locations that will draw a crowd, set up one or more small group discussions with potential program participants. Marketing experts call these "focus groups." For example, statistical data indicated that 22 families in the Central church and 413 in its ministry area had children under 6 years of age. In surveys, 65 percent of these expressed interest in attending parenting classes. So to get more specific information, a group interview was set up with two couples and two single parents with preschool children. One couple and one single parent were church members; the others were not. A church member led the discussion, using a detailed list of questions compiled by the planning committee. A second church member sat in on the discussion and took notes. This method not only helps gather information; it also builds interest in the program under consideration.

Targeting Your Ministry

When you have defined the needs, you can begin to define the target group for a new ministry. Remember that the specific group of people you are seeking to minister to is the reason for the entire effort. Real, Christ-centered, Spirit-led ministry is not organized because churches ought to have activities and look alive, but rather because "people need the Lord"—people who suffer, who seek answers, who search for support and friendship. Relational ministry is about people, not programs. Who are the people we want to contact, get acquainted with, and build lasting relationships with?

There is a temptation to be very unrealistic about this question.

On most occasions when I sit as a consultant with a group starting a new ministry and ask, "Whom are you trying to reach?" the answer is either a variation of "everybody" or "anybody." Both answers can lead to failure. An "anybody" focus is a failure to see the forest because of total attention on one or two trees. Excellent ministry may happen with a handful of individuals, but a group ministry capable of reaching a significant number of other needy souls will not be built. An "everybody" focus is a failure to see trees because of total attention on the forest. Unrealistic estimates of how many people can actually be touched can lead to discouragement and make those who do respond feel like they are not really cared for as individuals, but are valued only as chips in the pile.

Douglas W. Johnson, director of the Institute for Church Development, gives a realistic formula for calculating how many people might be reached through a new ministry. Start with the number of persons in the target group as given by the census data, and multiply this figure by the percentage that Adventists represent among the total church members in the community. This is usually between .5 and 2 percent. Next, add the number of church members who are in the same category.

For example, if you were launching a singles ministry, you might calculate the target audience this way: Let's suppose your community has 10,250 single adults, your church represents 1 percent of the total churched people in town, and you have 40 single adults in your congregation. The figures would look like this:

$$10,250 \times .01 + 40 = 142 \text{ persons}$$

This would be the number of people you could reasonably expect to reach with your new ministry. Johnson says, "On top of this figure may be added a goal that represents the number of members of the target group the congregation will work to involve." Current research in group dynamics indicates that an ongoing group or seminar will enroll no more than 40 people. If a church expects to involve more than 40 participants in a new ministry, it must design a program with several groups, perhaps meeting on different nights or on different schedules or in different locations.

The Ministry Team

The coordinator for the new ministry need not be an expert or a professional, but it is essential that this person have ability in organizing and carrying through projects, and have the trust of the target audience and the church board. The coordinator need not be one of the target group, but she or he must be able to communicate with the target group. She or he should be an individual with a clear commitment to the church and to Christ, and a willingness to see this ministry as a long-term activity, an opportunity to learn new skills and be exposed to new ideas. It is foolish to move ahead without this. Even if you must wait for a qualified individual to develop this sense of call, the investment of time will eventually pay off in a ministry with a strong spiritual base, quality programming, and skilled leadership.

The coordinator will need a supportive team of volunteers. The size of the target audience and the anticipated program will indicate how large a team, but at least four specific roles must be filled. You will want two working assistants—one to deal with paperwork, purchasing, setting up equipment, making phone calls, distributing advertising, etc.; and another to chat with people as they gather at events, to get to know them personally, answer questions, be available to listen, and set up personal visits outside the group activities. And you will need two "behind the scenes" supporters—one (possibly the pastor or an elder) to serve as an administrative counselor and a channel of communication between the ministry team and the church board; the other to rally intercessory prayer on behalf of the venture. The entire team should meet monthly or quarterly for evaluation, prayer, brainstorming, planning, sharing, and caring for one another. The quality of relationships within this team will determine to a large degree the success of the ministry.

Developing the Details

When you have defined the needs and the target group, you can begin to put together a specific plan of action for a new ministry. The church board should authorize a planning committee to put on paper (and bring back to the board for consideration) a proposal that includes a specific description of the needs and the target audience, the objectives, the ministry coordinator and team, program design, curriculum resources, budget, and suggested starting date.

For an effective ministry, program content must clearly and helpfully address the needs expressed by the target audience. But "packaging" is also vital. Where will the group or groups meet? Where the Adventist church is well known and perceived positively, suitable meeting rooms at the church itself may be best. But sometimes the program will get off to a better start if you use the Y, a local bank, or some other public facility. Often you can secure such community rooms without charge, but even if not, to have a comfortable meeting room at a recognized address is usually well worth the cost.

What time of year will the first seminar or fellowship be scheduled? Every community has favorable seasons, and seasons also when low attendance is guaranteed. For example, one church in Pennsylvania offered a health screening event on the weekend that the football season came to its climax. Few came out. The same program, with the same advertising, in the same location a year earlier during the spring attracted 10 times as many people.

When will the group or groups meet? A fellowship for young mothers might best meet on a weekday at midmorning. A teen/parent support group might work well on Saturday afternoons. A group of couples might need to be over by 8:30 p.m., while a singles group might flourish by starting about 8:00 p.m. And how many times will the group meet? Although one-shot events (all day or a weekend) would seem to make it easier for more people to be present, educational research indicates that for a program to have significant impact (especially in changing habits or attitudes), a number of sessions over several weeks is necessary. Lyman

Coleman, author of the *Serendipity* materials for small groups, says that people will attend 6 to 10 weekly sessions more readily than 12 to 40 weekly sessions, and he points out that if a "beginners' group" is rewarding, people may be willing to take a more extended commitment. Also, groups that meet every other week can be as effective as weekly sessions if the number of sessions remains the same.

The more amenities included, the more attractive a group or seminar becomes. Something to drink, refreshments during a break, a notebook or folder, pencils and notepads, audiovisuals and handouts, and name badges make the program more attractive and professional. See that participants have an opportunity to mix and get acquainted. Clearly identify in your printed materials the sponsoring organization and the staff, so that further contacts can be made and questions asked.

With some target groups, child care is a crucial service. Young couples, parents—and especially single parents—cannot be expected to attend a fellowship or seminar if child care is not provided. Grandparents and older brothers and sisters are almost never able to watch the children. Baby-sitters are difficult to find and costly. Quality child care is essential in your planning even if this means a slightly higher registration fee. Church volunteers are not your only source for child care, although this may be an ideal way to involve a teenage girl or a grandmother who feels she does not have other skills. You can also pay people for this service. The cost of a single baby-sitter for six couples is far less than all six getting individual baby-sitters. Use qualified non-Adventists if the available pool of Adventist volunteers is involved in other tasks.

Curriculum Resources

One reason that target group ministries are within reach of every Adventist church, no matter how small, is that a vast number of curriculum resources have been published recently. Most have detailed guides for the group leader and textbooks or other materials for the participants. More recently, Adventist Life Seminars has begun to produce packages that include videotape lectures by such well-known Adventist speakers as Dr. Kay Kuzma. (The *NAD Resource Catalog* is the reference book for available resources.)

Many of the published curriculum resources use inexpensive audiovisuals, overheads you can reproduce on a photocopy machine, flipcharts, etc. The planning group must choose which curriculum resources to use, whether to follow one (perhaps in modified form) or to use two or three curricula together. Ask these questions, too: What supplies must be ordered? How long does shipment take? What are the policies concerning minimum orders and returning unused materials? Never plan to start the group, see who shows up, and then order materials. That appears inept to participants and guarantees a large number of unused materials.

Guest speakers can be used, even within the framework of a curriculum outline. For example, a nurse may teach one unit and the pastor another, instead of one instructor doing the whole thing. Karen Spruill, director of the Mother's Center at the Battle Creek Tabernacle, uses guest speakers exclusively in her ministry. "You may be surprised at all the speakers you can think of," she says. "Who are the professionals in your congregation, and where do they work? Who are the respected women leaders in your town and church? Who are the women who have raised successful children, who have interesting hobbies or businesses? Start a list of programs that you have seen offered in the newspaper, or by continuing education classes at the local colleges. Become familiar with the United Way agencies."

Writing Objectives and Budget

No plan is complete unless it includes a simple, specific description of expected results. What is the desired effect on those who attend? What are the criteria for success? You need to list expectations precisely, not to satisfy academic or bureaucratic urges but to help the team, the church board, and others involved to understand clearly what your ministry seeks to achieve. This list keeps the ministry moving in the right direction and keeps the leaders honest. Grammar, language, even correct spelling, are not essential in writing a good objective. Three considerations are fundamental, however:

1. Make it specific, not general.
2. Make it something doable, not abstract.
3. Make it measurable.

When you have reached this point, the planning committee can then work out a budget and schedule for the new ministry. The schedule provides specific deadlines for maintaining accountability, and the budget provides for realistic funding. This ought to include income generated by the ministry through registration fees, offerings at meetings, specially solicited donations, membership dues, etc., as well as a subsidy from the church budget.

Unless there is something specific about your target group that indicates otherwise, don't be afraid to charge fees for some programs. The public usually considers "free" programs to have some kind of payoff or ulterior motive, and is justifiably unwilling to get involved. (What was your response the last time you got one of those "free trip to Florida" offers in the mail?) When programs are offered to the public with a modest registration fee or charge for materials, it enhances the public image of the program and makes it appear more professional. Charging a fee will actually increase enrollment in most circumstances. There are obvious exceptions to this rule among low-income and some other target groups.

You will now have a document describing the needs, the target audience, the program design and curriculum, the specific objectives of the ministry, and its working team, budget, and schedule, which you can present to the church board. After the board has voted approval, you can introduce the team during a Sabbath morning worship and in prayer "set them aside" or consecrate them to their new ministry. Now they must begin to communicate with the target audience.

Marketing Your Ministry

The team has many mediums of communication from which to select. They must choose carefully which to use. The situation in a specific local community, the kind of people they are trying to reach, and financial considerations all come into play. In any case, they will have to pay for some of the publicity. They cannot rely on free advertising to produce results, although they should use free publicity in community newspapers and public-service announcements on radio and television stations to supplement the major advertising items.

The available mediums for communication can be divided into three major categories: relational media, which feature person-to-person contact; formal media, such as direct mail; and public media, such as the newspapers and broadcasting facilities. Both small towns and target groups with low levels of education can best be reached through relational communication. Suburban areas, especially white collar communities, are best contacted through formal means. And the public media most effectively penetrate the highly urbanized areas. The level of education, lifestyle, and residential area of the target audience will indicate what choices must be made in designing the advertising campaign for a particular ministry.

Relational media are simply organized ways of using word of mouth. Of course, word-of-mouth advertising is always helpful and not very costly. One can initiate an informal advertising effort simply by carefully informing the congregation on Sabbath morning and urging them to tell their friends, neighbors, and work associates. Better organized and more effective means include setting up telephone committees, going door-to-door to distribute information in housing developments with high concentrations of the target audience, and arranging to make in-person announcements at community meetings of various kinds. Relational media will be much more effective if one reinforces them with a well-done brochure of some kind—a handout to back up the word-of-mouth communication. Relational media cost little in terms of money but much in volunteer hours. Boards sometimes too easily decide to "save money" by relying on relational media while taking no responsibility for providing the many volunteer hours necessary to implement their decision.

Formal media are probably the most cost-effective forms of advertising available to local churches. Of these, mass mailings—the kind of mailing addressed to "Resident" and usually done by a professional mail advertising company—are more costly and less effective than other types of mailings. However, they can be useful in getting public attention for a new ministry in a community where the church has not developed much contact over the years, or when the target audience is a group that has been unreached in the past. Since the response rate is usually about one percent, you must mail many thousands of pieces; and this can be very costly.

Direct mail differs from mass mailing in that it is sent to specific addressees by name. These names may be obtained from a direct mail company according to your target audience, or from lists of people the church has contacted in one way or another over the years. For example, It Is Written, Faith for Today, and the Voice of Prophecy can supply the names and addresses of people in specified zip code areas who have requested booklets on the specified topics over the past three or four years. If the interest coordinator in your church has been systematically keeping a file of interested persons, this becomes a gold mine for advertising new ministries. Steve Dunkin has developed an effective, simple manual of procedures for local churches who want to do their own direct-mail advertising at low cost.[5]

Public media are the most expensive forms of communication and the most difficult to utilize. When a ministry decides to purchase ads in a newspaper or spots on a radio station, it should also seek professional counsel from someone other than the sales-people at the publishing or broadcasting company; otherwise they risk wasting large sums of money. Public advertising is so highly complex and sophisticated that even professionals fail more often than they succeed, especially in the marketing of services or entertainment. And few advertising professionals understand the unique factors involved in marketing a ministry.

Where can local church members get good advice without spending money on consulting fees? First, try to set up an appointment with one of the best public relations firms in the area. These professionals often are willing to give one or two consultations at no charge for a volunteer, community service effort with a small budget. Second, see if the United Way or a major local nonprofit institution has a professional public relations director. This individual would not charge a fee for some advice and is often extremely knowledgeable. Finally, perhaps the church can find and obtain the aid of an Adventist public relations professional. These people are often willing to assist local churches that want to do something creative in the public media.

Perhaps one of the greatest misunderstandings concerning advertising involves searching for "the best method." All communication experts agree that there is no one best method of advertising. Successful advertising always uses a mix of several media. When a local church is communicating with a target audience outside its congregation, it will need to put out a minimum of six different kinds of advertising. For example, your ministry might choose to utilize: (1) word of mouth by the congregation; (2) a telephone committee to contact those the media ministries (Faith for Today, etc.) indicate might be interested; (3) door-to-door distribution of a printed flyer in several apartment complexes with high concentrations of the target audience; (4) a mailing to the names in the church interest file; (5) a mailing to relevant professionals in the area; and (6) posters in supermarkets and laundromats. Of course, the specific mix used in each local situation must be based on the nature of the target audience, the funds available, the volunteer manpower available, and local ways of doing things.

You have not completed the marketing task when the first public program has been held and a crowd has come out. You must utilize continuing, supportive advertising to keep those who have responded coming back. For instance, you might use a telephone committee to remind participants of each monthly fellowship or publish a newsletter.

Ministering to Individuals

You have a group of 35 enthusiastic people at your monthly singles fellowship. They regularly make appreciative comments. You've been receiving phone calls from people who want to know how they can join the group. In short, the new singles ministry seems like a success. But is it? Not if there are no close, personal relationships developing between the people attending and the ministry team. It is this most important dimension that makes it truly a relational ministry.

It is easy to somehow lose sight of this fundamental element of ministry even when the team includes outgoing, naturally friendly people who are enthusiastic and "bubbly." Exciting, entertaining public relationships and rewarding, meaningful personal relationships are two different things. In order to minister effectively to people, one must get beyond superficial, friendly contacts and hear their deep, inner concerns. Only at this intimate level can spiritual needs be identified and met. The relational skills necessary to reach people in this interior, spiritual part of their lives are the skills that give appropriate experiential reality to the "message" of a ministry.

If what you are doing is to be a relational ministry and not just a church program, then one or more individuals on the team must have the depth listening skills to work with people at the level of their spiritual needs (see chapter 3). Ideally, the entire team should have this kind of training and awareness. The Friendship Evangelism Seminar and the advanced 40-hour listening lab are perhaps the best training experiences currently available for the development of these skills. Many Adventists are certified to teach these courses. (You can call the NAD Church Ministries office to get the names of qualified Adventist trainers in your area.) Similar training programs have begun to be created, such as the Stephen Series, an interdenominational project, and the new videos and workbooks being developed by the Harvest 90 Adventist Research Taskforce.

Pastors who want to enable their people to minister effectively and to move their congregation into a relational approach to evangelism will arrange for this kind of training. These are the key skills that make it possible to share the gospel with unchurched people in a relational way. They can be described in books and on tapes, but they can be learned only in hands-on situations in which it is possible to demonstrate and practice live behaviors.

Creating Pathways Into Church Fellowship

Conducting "touch" ministries simply as "bait" to lure people into church membership is manipulative and un-Christlike. But it is equally irresponsible and sub-Christian to conduct ministries in such a way as to create barriers for participants who want to satisfy their spiritual needs by participating in the caring fellowship and celebrative worship of the sponsoring church. The growing church will open clear pathways for those who wish to move from specialized ministries into closer fellowship with the congregation. Availability, accessibility, genuine caring, and effective specialized ministries will lead to voluntary contacts by individuals and families interested in sampling the religious activities of the church.

Unchurched people decide to make a first visit to a church when motivated by such occurrences as a divorce, birth of a child, and other "life events." An effective target group ministry touches many unchurched people who are experiencing these life events, and some of these people will think about visiting the church from which the ministry team comes that has demonstrated its concern and friendship. If members of the team are using depth listening skills, they will hear these spiritual needs being expressed and will be able to refer people to appropriate spiritual activities that the church offers.

As I said in the previous chapter, small Bible study and support groups afford one of the most effective pathways to church fellowship for unchurched people. Interested people contacted through an outreach can be referred to these groups for further growth and spiritual nurture. Better yet, an evangelistic Bible study group should be built into the ministry itself. Every specialized ministry should be a discipling ministry and a teaching ministry, as well as a reaching ministry.

Some personalities are not comfortable in small groups, and will need ongoing fellowship and instruction in the form of one-to-one Bible studies. Every congregation has members who are gifted in personal evangelism. In order to follow through effectively, these "lay Bible ministers" will need some orientation to the activities of the specialized ministry with which the interested individuals have been involved. Members of the ministry team should set up these kinds of contacts through introductions and gentle steering.

A congregation can make the unchurched participants in their specialized ministries feel welcome in worship by having periodic special Sabbaths. One church held a "Rededication to Fathering," which 32 nonmember fathers attended. Many churches cosponsor a "Singles Weekend" with Adventist Singles Ministries. A "Rebounding From Rejection" sermon series could appeal to divorce recovery participants and those in a support group for the unemployed. The church could invite outstanding guest speakers on relevant topics for the worship hour and then conduct a two- or three-hour seminar after lunch. By mailing an appropriate invitation to all previous participants in related specialized ministries, and putting a telephone committee to work, the church can ensure a significant number of visitors on special Sabbaths. The same principle applies to public evangelistic meetings. The skill of the preacher in relating the target group needs to the Bible will determine whether or not these people come back to hear more of the gospel.

Unfortunately, churches can be very effective at screening out people they do not want as part of their fellowship. Unchurched people who visit church because of a specialized ministry are likely to be turned away on their first visit unless the congregation has made specific preparations to prevent this. Is your church "user friendly" to the target audience? For example, if your church is offering parenting seminars to the public, do parents who visit find easily accessible child-care facilities? Does the congregation accept noisy, untrained preschoolers? If the church is conducting a singles ministry, do single adults who visit find a couple-oriented set of announcements in the bulletin? The church leadership needs to think through carefully what a target-audience person would find during a first visit to the church, and clear the "mine field" in advance.

The ministry of hospitality as exercised by the greeters, ushers, and other lay leaders helps determine whether or not first-time visitors come a second time. Other key considerations include these: Is the building accessible? Is ample parking available close to the entrance? Are the people warm and open? Does the style of worship fit the cognitive style of the visitor? (For example, will highly kinesthetic people find opportunity to shake hands during the worship service and interact with the pastor? Will highly visual people find visual aids used in worship?) Is the music within the experience and idiom of the age group and cultural background of the visitor? Is there a comfortable class for the first-time attender at Sabbath School? Do parents find the kind of children's program they want? Are people invited to dinner, either in a home or at the church? New people should not get a visit or telephone call until they have attended worship two or three times. Making contact sooner will usually be seen as being too aggressive, unless the person is a former Adventist or an Adventist who has recently moved into the area.

As the first-time visitor returns, other essential elements are important in continuing their spiritual growth. Do the pastor's sermons speak to his or her needs? Does the music and liturgy give him a sense of hope and encouragement and joy? Does the Sabbath

School teach people how to apply the Bible to everyday problems and questions? Are there opportunities to openly discuss frustrations, concerns, and decisions in confidential, supportive groups? Will church friends stick with the potential member through crisis and misconduct, through pain and joy? Is the possibility of God's being present, loving, and meaningful in his life apparent because of the way He is shared, pictured, and spoken of by church friends? Is faith sustained through the struggles of life; does this "family of faith" help its people cope with life? Through it all, is the specialized ministry a seamless part of the total church experience so that there is a natural progression from participation as an unchurched person in the specialized, needs-serving ministry to participation as a church member in joyous Sabbath worship of the Lord? These critical questions make the difference between a church that really ministers to people and a church that does not.

1. L. Paul Jensen, "Campus Ministry in Orange County," *Meeting the Secular Mind: Some Adventist Perspectives* (Berrien Springs, Mich.: Andrews University Press, 1987), pp. 174, 175.
2. M. Coyner, "Why People Join."
3. Kermit Netteburg et al., *North American Division Marketing Program,* vol. 1, pp. 49, 59.
4. Produced by the Pacific Union Conference Church Ministries Department and available through the NAD Distribution Center, 5040 Prescott, Lincoln, Nebraska 68506.
5. Steve Dunkin, *Church Advertising* (Nashville: Abingdon Press, 1982).

CHAPTER 10
Mobilizing the Laity for Ministry

A FTER MORE than a decade of emphasis on spiritual gifts, the new generation of Adventist pastors in North America is convinced that the laity must become involved in the ministry of the church. Indeed, they often preach the scriptures that state plainly that each member of the body of Christ has been given a special gift for ministry, which, when discovered and utilized properly, builds up the church (see Eph. 4; Rom. 12; 1 Cor. 12). Yet when it comes to actual practice, it often seems easier and quicker for the pastor to attempt to do the work of ministry himself or herself than to equip and train the church members to share it.

This has become increasingly true during the 1980s as the average household invests more and more of its time in occupational responsibilities. Three out of four women under 50 work outside the home, and most of these have a "second shift" of housekeeping, too. This has been shown to be true in surveys of Adventist women, as well as in the general public. The average workweek in the United States has moved from 39 hours in the 1970s to 47 hours in the 1980s. And as the supply of "free time" decreases, there is greater competition for it—more recreation, hobby, and cultural opportunities are constantly being generated.

As it becomes more difficult to get helpers, the tendency is to pile more and more on a handful of long-term faithful workers in each congregation; to feel that "we don't have time for a devotional or lengthy prayer during committee meetings." Increasingly, lay leaders in local churches feel burned out, and some drop out of the church because of these feelings. An interdenominational survey of Protestant church lay leaders asked directly if they were "burned out as a leader in the parish." More than half responded in the positive. Only a third said burnout was clearly not a problem. I have replicated this study in several Adventist congregations, and found the same or a more alarming response. These surveys were validated by administering a standard 32-question instrument based on major symptoms identified by social scientists working with the issue of burnout.

There is a profound negative effect on congregational life "when one out of four key lay leaders is exhausted, cynical, disillusioned, and self-deprecating," says Roy Oswald, director of the interdenominational study. He asks: "Is this a reason that morale in some congregations is low? Is this one of the reasons that some congregations fail to grow?" He places this issue in a theological perspective. "The church's primary ministry is with people and to people. In order to be effective the church, must use its own human resources. What is the church's record in the stewardship of its human resources? How well does the church care for the people who give primary energy to sustaining its institutional work?"

Although neither Oswald's research nor mine among Adventist churches is based on a large enough sample to be conclusive, they do give some hints as to why there is such a high degree of exhaustion and negative attitudes among lay leaders. These people are very busy in every aspect of their lives. Not only do they volunteer one or two evenings a week at the church, but they are heavily involved in other civic, family, and business activities. They are the doers of the church and the community.

Another reason for burnout among lay leaders has to do with the realities of parish life to which they are exposed. "When one is pulled more deeply into the center of parish life," says Oswald, "one may develop greater negativism toward fellow parishioners. About half of those in the study indicated that when they became a parish leader they became more aware of the pettiness and backbiting of some church members, and nearly 40 percent say that they find themselves becoming cynical because fellow church members often do not follow through on what they say they will do in church activities. This is slightly more pronounced in the Adventist churches I've studied than in Oswald's Protestant sample.

The self-absorption, materialism, and ambition that have become dominant trends in North American culture not only make people less interested in volunteering but explain the new demands made when people do agree to volunteer. They want clear and limited tasks, short terms in office, plenty of manpower to use in attaining the program goal, and simple, direct feedback about how they are doing, including lots of affirmation. About a quarter of the respondents in Oswald's study complained of the lack of definite job descriptions; more than half said that they have difficulty with the expectation that they will do a certain job in the church year after year. Nearly 70 percent said that it was untrue for them that normally they have all the resources (people, money, etc.) they need to do their job in the parish, and 40 percent reported that they often feel overloaded because they try to do it all themselves. One out of four said they often have difficulty delegating work to others in the church and holding them accountable for the jobs they have accepted. In my surveys, Adventist lay leaders indicated the same response.

Lay leaders report that they do not get very much feedback from the church or the pastor once they accept a responsibility and begin to carry it out. Although the majority agree that they are often complimented or shown appreciation for their work in the church, very few report that they get some kind of evaluation or review of how they are doing with their responsibilities. Many felt that either no one really cared what kind of job they did, or that the job was not really very important, because of the lack of monitoring and review.

The largest single cause of burnout identified by lay leaders in both studies is sitting through many frustrating meetings. Only one in 10 said that it was not true that "I often find myself frustrated at the conclusion of a parish meeting." They feel that most of the time in church-related committees and boards is wasted. Pastors and others responsible for setting up meetings need to give much more attention to the basics: clear purpose for the meeting, carefully prepared agenda, adequate homework done in advance, written reports with all the background facts necessary to make decisions, etc. Meetings should not be held unless there is a real need that can be simply and clearly stated. Careless inattention to these basic elements of leadership is costing the church rich resources in manpower and spiritual commitment.

Both studies suggest several things that pastors and lay leaders can begin to do about the problem of burnout among church volunteers. "An excellent place to begin is for a parish to have one or two individuals conduct an exit interview with all people leaving major roles," says Oswald. He suggests that questions like these be asked . . .

What was the most difficult aspect of the role, and what was most enjoyable and satisfying about the work?

What are your recollections of major achievements?

What initial hopes and expectations did you need to relinquish?

What are the issues that your successor will need to face?

What are the key problems ahead for the parish as seen from your perspective?

If you could do the job over again, what would you do differently?

What are your feelings about leaving this position?

Specific needs in a particular local church will emerge as these interviews are conducted and the results collected. Other issues that need to be considered will include more ways of saying thank-you to church volunteers; greater attention to assessment of the spiritual gifts of church members; avoiding the tendency to overprogram the church; providing opportunities for spiritual renewal for key lay leaders; and specific procedures for recruiting volunteers, with clear arrangements for a simple, written "contract," training, supervision, and evaluation.[1]

The church is up against powerful and sophisticated competitive forces when it seeks the involvement of its members in ministry. It must become more intentional and competent in recruiting, placing, training, supporting, and managing volunteers. The heavy-handed attempts at guilt and manipulation that have been traditionally used will no longer work. "Everyone who has heard the gospel wants to obey God's call . . . . Motivation is not whipping people up into action. It is channeling their own desires into bridges that lead to success."[2]

The essential elements of an adequate program using volunteers in ministry include:

1. A sense of community and the opportunity for developing friendships with other volunteers.

2. A chance for personal growth and development.

3. Participation by volunteers in problem solving and significant decision-making.

4. Choosing from involvement alternatives related to individual interests and needs.

5. An explicit contract regarding time and level of commitment.

6. Opportunity to help set goals.

7. Regular mechanisms for affirmation and feedback.

8. Meaningful orientation and training activities.

The few effective tools for equipping members to minister usually have two fatal flaws—they require either too little from the lay minister or too much from the pastor. It is easy to make lay ministry too simple, to ask the motivated church member who truly wants to share in the mission of the church to do something so simplistic that it quickly becomes boring and kills enthusiasm. Every member of the congregation is asked to do the same mechanical, repetitive job that neither engages the imagination nor the commitment of those involved. Often no attempt is made to match tasks with the gifts of individuals.

On the other hand, those lay ministry programs that require a degree of professionalism and serious engagement usually insist on a large amount of involvement and supervision from the pastor. Training through tutorial or coaching processes is often demanded, necessitating an unrealistic amount of time out of the pastor's schedule. In fact, the major reason such programs are not put to greater use in the church is because of the slow start necessitated by the commitment of so much pastoral time.

To be usable, a lay ministry program should give both the pastor and the people a certain amount of freedom, while maintaining a necessary degree of organization. Church members should be free to work in areas where their gifts provide the needed motivation, and they should be free to develop activities and goals at their own pace without having to wait on their pastor's schedule. Pastors should be freed of a growing burden of administrative minutia, so that they can give spiritual and emotional support to the efforts of the lay ministers. At the same time the ministries of laity and clergy must come together as a unified whole—a strategy that knits together the separate roles played by different members of one team. Experience has shown that the use of small groups within the congregation is the most successful means of meeting these criteria.

Small groups provide the breadth of opportunity necessary to deal with the many different gifts that people have, and they also allow for leadership to be delegated so that the pastor does not have to do all the training, supervising and managing. In my experience, when a small group strategy has been pursued for at least two years, the congregation has experienced unprecedented growth both in numbers and in the spiritual life of the members.

Despite the ideal nature of the small group approach, many congregations that try to initiate it do experience certain problems.

Groups can become exclusive instead of inclusive—so centered on Bible study and fellowship that they make no attempt to attract outsiders. Newcomers may feel as if they are intruding. Groups can become scenes for conflict rather than concerted action—so heterogeneous that goals cannot be agreed upon. The promise held out by the small group concept has soured in the minds of many because of these problems.

Difficulty in implementing the small group approach can usually be traced to three items. First, the groups are begun with little or no preparation or education. Second, everyone is expected to participate. Third, groups are assigned from a list instead of allowing individuals to group themselves around goals and natural clusters voluntarily. To be effective a small group strategy must provide adequate orientation for people before they move into groups, and must keep the groups mission-centered and voluntary.

A design that takes these factors into consideration has been developed and field-tested in scores of Adventist congregations over the past decade. I call it a "workshop for mission,"[3] and a leader's guide is available free by writing to me at the NAD office, 12501 Old Columbia Pike, Silver Spring, Md. 20904. (Mark Finley has written a similar package entitled *The Adventist Way to Church Growth*, which is published by Concerned Communications.) This design includes about 10 weekly sessions, and ends with a weekend or one-day retreat. It can easily be implemented during midweek meetings, Sabbath afternoons, or even Sabbath mornings. As a result of this process, between 10 and 25 percent of the church membership can be expected to become involved in active, ministering small groups.

The Enabling Process

Each of the weekly sessions involves 90 minutes to two hours, including Bible study, discussion, lab learning exercises, and time for review and questions. Readings can be assigned between classes or incorporated into introductory presentations.

The pastor's role in these sessions must be that of a facilitator, not a lecturer. That is why it is best for the "lecture" information to be given through reading assignments. Much of the learning is experiential and comes from the open discussions and the lab sessions. It is more important to get a general feel for the nature of a good small group ministry than to learn specific skills.

The emphasis throughout the series is that these are working sessions, moving toward an action program of small group ministries. I have found it best to combine "training" with actual preparation for the small group program to be implemented by the church. In fact, the small group strategy of the congregation is designed in the workshop sessions. Nevertheless, some of those who attend the sessions will intend simply to hear and learn without any intention of getting involved in the program. It should be made clear repeatedly during the series that those who actually do not want to join small groups are welcome, and that this is actually a testing period for people to "try out" the small group idea and see if they like it. But it should also be pointed out that those who actually do not plan to participate will be expected to drop out at a time to be announced at one of the last sessions. In the meantime, all those in attendance will be expected to participate in the discussions and labs. "Sitting out" a lab exercise is unfair to those participating.

The Retreat

The retreat becomes even more fully a working session. During this time the small groups actually meet in their more permanent form for the first time to set goals and minimum requirements for themselves. They are asked to write a statement of mission, including a definition of their target audience and the specific approach they are going to use as they initiate their ministry.

In the retreat environment the groups are asked to do their planning with a deep awareness of the presence of the Holy Spirit. Time for meditation and prayer is essential so that the plans of the groups are a result of really listening for God's call in their lives and not just human constructions. Here the spiritual leadership demanded of the pastor will reach the highest level. Preaching the Word will be essential, but much greater time must be put into leadership of silent meditation and prayer sessions that are not routine.

At the retreat it is also essential that the pastor "let go" of the groups. The groups will have to spend a good portion of this time without the presence of the pastor, meeting separately and taking on a life of their own. The rule should be announced that in keeping with his role as facilitator, the pastor will come into a group meeting only when invited, and only when a very specific request for help has been framed by the group. There will be a real temptation for the pastor to overcontrol this process. He or she can resist that temptation by spending time in prayer and meditation while the groups have their planning meetings.

During the initial field testing of the "workshop for mission" design, eight congregations organized more than 50 small groups. Large and small churches; Black, White, and Hispanic congregations; and churches located in small, rural towns and large cities were included. A number of these groups met only a few times on their own and accomplished little or nothing. Several groups functioned for more than a year and engaged in active outreach programs. In two cases they helped to plant new churches in unreached communities. One group developed a prison ministry, and two conducted extensive health ministries. Another group developed a college-level training center that became affiliated with a denominational institution. Significant numbers of baptisms resulted.

Not every group is going to survive. Not every group is going to be truly creative. But the power of the Holy Spirit working through lay ministries will be released, and growth, excitement, and renewal will be seen.

What About Committees?

The small group and the committee tend to appeal to different kinds of personalities. "Relational people aren't motivated by tradition or denominational loyalty," says Roberta Hestenes. "They want to know, *Will this activity give me a meaningful, authentic, significant experience?* They want to feel they count as individuals. They want their personal concerns recognized. A task-oriented committee usually feels, to them, cold and impersonal. Program-oriented people, on the other hand, tend to hold an older view that sees talking about yourself and your problems as boorish and impolite.... [They] see themselves ... as selflessly getting things done. To them, the bottom line for a committee is What have we accomplished and how much did it cost?

"When one group finds fulfillment through relationships and the other through the exercise of power, tension between the two is inevitable. The people trying to keep the institution on course will become increasingly discouraged about not having enough money, resources, or support for what they are doing. The relational people will build small group networks and attract people who find these groups meaningful. But as the church begins to grow (and with it, demands on the program), the institutional people will ask why the relational people don't get with the program."[4]

Dr. Hestenes points out that the major drawback of the traditional church committee is that often the members do not expect to do any work, but come merely to listen to what is proposed, give their opinion, and vote it up or down. Self-centered, feel-good cliques that began as small group ministries can be just as unproductive. She advocates "mission-focused" groups that work to accomplish a ministry to others outside the group and to take care of one another within the group under the leadership of Christ's Word and the guidance of the Holy Spirit. How can that happen in your committees? Seven steps are important:

1. Choose leaders who already demonstrate ministry in their lives and who have a vision for people as the purpose of programs. Recruit with care and honesty about expectations, job description, and the time it will take. Don't put people on a committee just

because they represent a traditional segment of the members who must be involved, or tell them they have to come only once a month for an hour. Make sure they understand that the basic responsibility of any group in the church is to generate a ministry, not run an organization. They are ultimately accountable to Christ's mission for the church, and theirs is a spiritual task. This kind of careful recruiting of committees takes more time than sitting around a table for three minutes putting together a list of names. Someone, often the pastor, has to meet with each person individually and slowly go over everything that is involved. Often a prayerful wait is necessary to get the right kind of decision.

2. Set the tone early with specific training activities at the first meeting of a new committee or a new year. For example, during the first meeting ask everyone to share something about how he or she first joined the Adventist Church. Help members make it a habit to begin each meeting with some kind of sharing question. Establish the expectation from the beginning that they will go away from every meeting with homework assignments, that significant, participatory prayer will be the norm, not trite, ritualistic invocations.

3. Have an annual retreat when the committee members can spend quality time in fellowship, Bible study, discussion of the theology and purpose of their mission, and long-range planning. Properly conducted—with lots of participatory exercises and few, if any, guest speakers—the retreat can provide spiritual and relational energy, as well as an action plan and budget for the coming year. This is where evaluation can happen, and personality clashes can be dealt with constructively. The undergirding spirituality of the group and its ministry is built in this setting, making it more than a ritual of traditional church activities, empowering it to make a difference in the lives of unchurched people in a secular world.

4. Meet in homes, take 15 minutes to help everyone "get on board" by sharing something that is happening to them this week. Start with the most important topics and move quickly through the agenda. End the evening with refreshments and informal conversation. That kind of regular committee meeting, together with a

printed agenda showing the actual timeframe mailed in advance, will bring high attendance, involvement, and commitment. Don't be afraid to cancel meetings when the leader is not prepared for them to be productive.

5. Have fewer "standing" committees and more short-term task forces. When a specific, tangible goal is to be accomplished, it should be put in the hands of a small group that will work on that one item for a few months until it is accomplished, and then go out of business. Permanent committees with broad responsibilities can keep a fix on the "big picture" and create subgroups as needed. These task forces can be hand-picked with the best people for the specific job at hand. Volunteers today respond best to very focused, time-limited assignments.

6. Add new people as gifts surface, not on some organizational schedule. All committee members should be empowered to recruit people they find to have an interest in the mission of the group. Fresh talent does not come along just in time for the annual nominating committee, nor do new people feel wanted when they must wait around until unexplained traditions indicate that the time has come to place them in a responsibility.

7. Teach committee chairpersons to see themselves as "undershepherds" of their "little flock." They should look for opportunities to care for their committee outside of the regular meetings. This should include little things like birthday and anniversary cards, relevant gifts of books and articles, and getting together for lunch, as well as the "big" times such as hospitalization, unemployment, graduations, weddings, funerals, etc. Help the chairpeople to develop listening skills and become sensitive to the personal side of their members so they can see how feelings, particularly spiritual feelings, impact the work of the committee, and how the committee experience impacts the spiritual growth and church relationships of committee members.

A growing number of Adventist churches across North America are implementing these ideas by organizing a church ministries council. The church ministries council is a merger of several committees and councils that local churches used to have, or are supposed to have, but that have suffered because of the "too many committees" problem. It combines the old Sabbath school council, lay activities (or personal ministries) council, and perhaps the youth council, family life council, stewardship committee, and others, depending on the size of the church.

Usually church boards spend most of their time on finances, the physical plant, and policy decisions. It has become an administrative body, not a ministry team. In many Adventist churches this results in no group giving real attention to people and ministry. As a result attendance drops, giving slides off, few special events and outreach projects are conducted, and the needs of members, as well as opportunities for growth are neglected. A church ministries council focuses on ministry rather than maintenance and money problems. It serves as the leadership team for the fellowship and ministries of the congregation, working to support and equip one another, as well as to respond to the needs in the congregation and surrounding community. When a church ministries council is formed in a church it is a chance to start fresh, establish a new pattern for group process and norms, and focus on new priorities. It has proved to be a vehicle for life and change in a congregation.

─────────────

1. Roy M. Oswald and Jackie McMakin, *How to Prevent Lay Leader Burnout* (Washington, D.C.: Alban Institute, Inc., 1984). This interdenominational study includes a kit which local churches can use for a survey of their own volunteers.

2. Roger L. Dudley and Des Cummings, Jr., *Adventures in Church Growth* (Hagerstown, Md.: Review and Herald Pub. Assn., 1983), p. 114.

3. Monte Sahlin, "Equipping Your Members to Minister," *Ministry*, February 1981.

4. Roberta Hestenes, "Turning Committees Into Community," *Leadership*, Summer Quarter 1989, pp. 46-52.

CHAPTER 11
Reinventing
the Local Church

T HERE ARE several different kinds of Adventist churches
in most large metropolitan areas. Very few Adventist congregations are classic "Old First" downtown churches
located in the central business district of a city. There are a number
of Adventist churches located in the inner city as well as in the
aging, working-class neighborhoods near the inner city. These
"blue-collar churches" are often ethnic congregations and sometimes quite resistant to growth and change. Many of the city
churches in the Adventist denomination are of the outer urban type,
located in a middle- or upper-class neighborhood toward the edge
of the central city where there are single-family homes and few, if
any, places of business, and serving a congregation that includes
both suburban and urban people. Many of these could be positioned
for significant growth. A few are quite large.

Except on the West Coast, Adventists have relatively few
suburban churches, and since this is where most of the White
population of North America is located, this may be one of the
reasons that the growth of White Adventist membership has
slowed. In fact, the best examples of fast-growing White churches
are located in suburbs, and an analysis of where net growth comes
from in local conferences indicates that it is largely from suburban
congregations. It is a myth that all Black or Hispanic churches are

inner-city churches. In fact, among Adventists most are of the blue-collar type, and some are outer-urban congregations with a middle-class style of ministry. Most of the other ethnic Adventist churches in North America are inner-city or blue-collar types of churches, with the greatest degree of poverty occurring among the most recent immigrants. These immigrant congregations account for nearly half of the net growth in the NAD.

By far the largest number of Adventist congregations in North America are located in small towns and rural communities. This is, in part, a reflection of the fact that half the Adventist membership lives in small towns and rural homes. This also reflects the failure of Adventist evangelization to penetrate the large cities effectively. While about one North American in five lives outside the major metropolitan areas, fully 50 percent of Adventist members live there. When innovations are developed to help church growth in the cities, resistance often comes from these "small churches." And the vast majority of them are small. In fact, most have been small so long that it is difficult to see how they will ever have significant growth. Two out of three Adventist churches in the NAD have less than 100 members, with an average Sabbath attendance of half that. Yet they include less than 20 percent of the total membership of the NAD. One of the reasons is that when a congregation has had fewer than 100 members for 40 years or longer, there is virtually no chance that it will ever have much growth.

The problems that confront small-town and rural churches have to do largely with the will to grow and with pastoral staffing. For two or three decades in many conferences the few large churches have subsidized through the tithe fund the provision of pastors among the small churches at a rate greater than otherwise would have been possible. In recent years, as tithe increases have slipped behind the rate of inflation and increasing percentages of the tithe have gone to school subsidies, it has no longer been possible to stick to a "two-church district" rule. Three- and four-church assignments are more common today. There is no evidence that this has had negative impact on church growth, nor have experiments with "one pastor per church" demonstrated that it will generate growth in small churches. What does seem to surface in many studies is the observation that small churches become comfortable with being small and tend to resist growing beyond the size where everyone can know all the members. Certain personalities need small churches, but can the Adventist Church staff them with pastors and continue its commitment to overseas missions and Christian education?

The problems that confront city churches are much the same across ethnic and racial lines. As one veteran Adventist urban minister points out: "The flight to the suburbs and beyond has drained the typical Adventist church in the city of much of its dynamic leadership and young adult constituency. . . . It is easy to conclude that there is apparently no way we can mount an offensive large enough to make a noticeable impact upon the large city. There is not enough money in the conference. There are not enough members. Therefore, it is assumed, we must be content to do the best we can until God mightily intervenes with the resourceful power of the Holy Spirit."[1] The typical city church includes a large number of senior citizens, broken families, religiously divided households, poor and uneducated folk, and a fair representation of the "walking wounded"—persons with disabling mental health problems. The members often commute from quite a distance and do not feel that they have the time to return to the church building for midweek activities. Often very few, if any, of the members live in the neighborhood where the church building is located. Many times they are viewed with hostility by the community, which should be the church's primary ministry area.

Faced with limited human and financial resources, what is the local church to do? The research indicates that a key element of growth is the adoption of goals about which the members feel a high degree of ownership. Assuming that the pastor and lay leaders want to see the church grow and want to accomplish more than simply going through the motions, how do they go about getting the congregation to think and pray through a new vision of who they are, and reposition the church? How might a local church pursue a search for increasing faithfulness and both qualitative and quantitative growth? A basic process of "vision to action" is described in this chapter, and some tangible scenarios are offered, after which some concrete data is shared concerning the results of a "visioning" process in which a consultant works with a congregation and helps it to become intentional about its future and its mission. Make no mistake about it, church growth is change! Evangelization is change! Before a church can grow, before it can evangelize a community, it must embrace change. Many of the changes involved in church growth are changes that must take place before high numbers of new members can be brought in. The qualitative aspects of growth precede the quantitative aspects. In a time when many define their religious experience as a way to hide out from the tremendous volume of change that is moving through our world today, it is not easy to get a congregation to change and grow.

How Church Renewal Begins

In order to grow and change, the leaders of a congregation must have both a vision of what their church can be and a blueprint to get there. It is always premature to begin planning for growth, to begin the discussion of long-range goals, without immersion of the entire process and the congregational leadership in quality time for prayer and study. A vision for growth and mission does not come without some "baptism" in ministry. That is why it is essential that the pastor begin with those who want to do something, begin to do some ministry, no matter how small, and then lay the groundwork for greater plans by holding up the example set in the first few small groups and ministries. This sets the stage for teaching from the pulpit the Bible's understanding of the purpose for which the church exists and the operational principles upon which it was founded. All during this "pre-work" it is essential that the pastor invite a few key people (those who already have a vision for ministry and growth) to join him or her in continual prayer—prayer that the concepts will be presented clearly and that the congregation will catch the same vision.

When the pastor hears discussion and prayer among a number of people in the congregation, when some experiments with small group ministries have already begun, when everyone has had opportunity to understand the Bible principles for church life, then and only then is it fruitful to begin a "visioning" process. This lack of spiritual preparation has defeated much of the emphasis on planning, "management by objectives," and local church goal-setting over the past decade.

The "visioning" sessions themselves can be as simple or sophisticated as the pastor and lay leaders feel is necessary. As I have typically conducted them, they consist of three to six meetings over one to six months, depending on the rate at which a congregation could digest the information and the change in thinking. Traditional planning processes in the church have revolved around the organization and implementation of programs. When we envision a repositioning of the church toward a relational evangelism, the focus moves to needs assessment, people flow, and a whole new vocabulary that may take some time for the congregation to get a grasp of. Nothing is to be gained by outrunning your key people. Each "visioning" session will include one or more of the following exercises:

1. A Season of Prayer. Careful, quality time in prayer is essential if the process is viewed as a tool through which God reveals His will for the congregation. The Holy Spirit is not at war with procedures for careful thinking. Instead, He uses them as arenas in which to call people to bold, risky ventures in mission and to see the hurt and need of people otherwise overlooked. There is an opinion popular in some quarters that it is more spiritual to operate intuitively with a seat-of-the-pants style of leadership, and that a life of real prayer in tune with the Holy Spirit is inimical to careful research and strategic planning. Nothing could be further from the truth. The really creative thinkers and careful planners throughout Christian history have been men and women who were very close to God. The God of the Scriptures is a God of order, clear objectives, and tremendous foresight. Prayer and planning fit more closely than any other two behaviors of which believers are capable.

2. Information. Before a congregation can clearly see God's will for its future, it must have a factual base on which to work. Excellent tools have been developed at the Institute of Church Ministry at Andrews University that enable any congregation to take an inexpensive survey of its members to assess its attitudes and resources for growth, and to get a profile of the people in its ministry area. Specialized data-gathering tools are also available for new members baptized in the last year, dropouts who have quit attending, and the attitudes of the general public in the neighborhood of the church. All of this gives a detailed picture of the people groups, their needs, and the present status of ministry to them. The "visioning" process begins with a careful look at this information through graphics and audiovisuals, as well as a discussion of what it means. This discussion can take the form of SWOT teams— groups of six that construct lists of the strengths, weaknesses, opportunities, and threats they see in the information about their church. After a half hour or 45 minutes, the SWOT teams come back together and pool their observations on a chalkboard or flipchart so that all can see.

3. Futures. What are some things you would like to see happen in our church over the next few years? The members are first asked this question individually and given some quiet time to jot down ideas on a large card or a sheet of paper. Then they are asked to find a partner and given about 10 to 15 minutes to exchange their papers and interview each other, pushing for more detail, more concrete ideas, more creative leaps, all the while taking notes. Finally, they are asked to move into groups of six. The papers are collected and each group is given a stack to read, discuss, and summarize on a sheet or two of poster paper. After about 45 minutes the groups are called together and the posters hung on the wall. What emerges is a picture of the future of the congregation as it is envisioned by the participating leaders or members. It may be jumbled a bit at first, but as duplicate items are eliminated and similar items combined from the several lists, a set of "owned goals" appears on the wall and excitement rises in the room. Additional brainstorming may result and new things be added to the list, or a more creative "twist" given to some things already on display.

4. Priorities. Not many congregations can realistically do all of the things they can think of to do, at least not all at once. So the possibilities collected in the previous exercise must now be weeded out. What are the two, three, or four key things that must be done in order for the congregation to move ahead most rapidly? Where should the congregational leaders focus? What outcomes will be most strategic in moving the church into new growth and news ministries? Prioritizing cannot be accomplished without some debate, but it can also get bogged down in a dialogue in which a few outspoken individuals hold the entire group at bay. Balloting techniques such as "forced pairing" allow a group to prioritize a number of options rapidly without becoming mired in counterproductive discussion. Sometimes major alternatives, like whether or not to sell a church facility and rebuild, require extended periods of discussion in order to be fair to all whose feelings and roots may be involved. More careful, step-by-step processes are needed in these instances. Remember that what is going on here is the "jelling" of fluid feelings and opinions, so it is important to maintain a concert of prayer throughout these discussions.

5. Doables. A nicely written mission statement or a set of exciting objectives will come to nothing if concrete action steps are not taken to implement them. Those steps must be conceived of and described before they can be taken. If more than a handful of people are to be involved in their implementation, then they must be written out for all to see and understand for themselves. The hardest work in the entire "visioning" process is writing out the detailed, step-by-step doables, along with specific deadlines, evaluative criteria, and cost factors. All of this is absolutely necessary, or the entire "vision" will come to nothing. Although this is where many people will want to drop out and delegate the work to some individual or small committee, remember that even the details will not be accepted if key people do not participate in their creation and buy into them. Perhaps the best plan is to have several smaller groups write doables at the same time, each taking a different segment of the total strategy, and then each report back to the entire group. Bottom line of the whole process is this: Does it change your calendar of activities, your list of church offices and committees, and your church budget? If there are no changes in the calendar and especially in the budget, then the congregation is not serious about change and is going nowhere.[2]

As scores of local churches have worked through this process, several alternative futures seem to emerge fairly often. They can be described as (1) repositioning the church, (2) revitalizing the church, (3) pastoral evangelism, (4) becoming an evangelistic center, (5) moving to the suburbs, and (6) planting a new church. Each has its own assets and liabilities, possibilities and threats. Each can be deceptive in its own way. Each demands dedication and hard work to achieve growth. Some options are more likely to reach out to the unchurched and baby boomers, others less likely. I will review each alternative briefly, and then share some data showing how this whole process of strategizing relates to church growth in a real experiment.

The Repositioning Alternative

In this option the pastor and key lay leaders work with the small portion of the church membership that is ready to make a major change in the worship style and ministry focus of the church, appealing to a new and different target audience than the congregation has attracted in the past. The emphasis here is on the development of human resources. The total effort of the pastor would be poured into building the quality of fellowship and collective witness in several intensive, small groups, developing the spiritual gifts of those members who choose to participate, and moving into targeted ministries.

During the first two years of this strategy, a church should expect to lose a significant portion of the existing membership. Many will leave because their comfortable routine has been upset by the nontraditional program, or they do not like the new style of worship and ministry necessary to reach out to a different target audience. In the third or fourth year, large gains in membership may appear as the new people flow catches on. The positive outcomes of this approach are the high visibility of a new style of worship, the quality of the lay witness, the rapid growth of a strong core of highly dedicated members reproducing in kind, and the cutting loose of the defeatist attitudes of the past. The negative results might include the anger of some members and even an initial slump in membership. In order for there to be any measure of success from this strategy, a church must have the understanding support of the conference administration and a pastor who is highly skilled in human relations and willing to take a strong leadership role.

The Revitalization Alternative

Where this option is pursued, the pastor involves the majority of the congregation in large group activities and working committees over a longer period of time, building a less intense but more widely shared sense of community and mission. The focus is on restoring life to the same basic pattern of outreach and nurture that the church has found effective in the past; serving the same "market." Leadership development is a priority in the church program. Instead of presenting a specific vision of the church and its mission, the pastor encourages the congregation to get together, talk it out, and write its own statement of mission. The church building may be a symbolic focus for this process, with almost everyone involved in refurbishing and repairing it. If it is a beautiful and historic building, it can easily be an asset in building community awareness and outreach.

When this is the direction a church selects, growth picks up very slowly, building steadily but not spectacularly. The positives about this alternative include the way in which the deteriorated situation is healed without making it seem worse, the strengthening of the congregation's support for conference and institutional programs such as a consolidated church school, and the conserving of existing resources. The negative factors in this option include the tremendous price tag attached to adequate restoration of an aging physical plant, the lack of numerical growth and evangelistic impact, and the long period of time required (four to six years) for such slim gains.

The Pastoral Evangelism Alternative

This strategy has long been a favorite way for Adventists to deal with churches that are "dying on the vine." In this approach the pastor uses most of his time in personal evangelism, schedules regular "reaping" meetings, and works largely by himself to produce an increase in baptisms as quickly as possible. He does not attempt to generate much activity on the part of the laity, although a few church members react to this plan with delight and offer to join in as volunteer assistants and take on some of the tasks required. Many of the members do little to help, other than to suggest former members and relatives for the pastor to visit and convert. In fact, in many cases the majority of the congregation look on cynically and complain quietly that the pastor is ignoring other problems. Some of the newly baptized people become active members and dynamic personalities that bring a small measure of revival to the rest of the members. Total membership will grow almost immediately by 1 or 2 percent a year, but there will be no increase in this growth rate over the years, and few pastors stay at it for long. The positive results in this option are the immediate and widely understood emphasis on "evangelism," the soul-winning impact, and the lack of conflict that comes when the topic of lay involvement is addressed as it is in other options. The negative results include the large number of dropouts that will move through the "back door," the lack of integrity in church membership, and the failure to deal with long-range problems.

Move to the Suburbs

The decision to sell an old building and construct a new physical plant in or near an area of fresh development is often seen as a way to bring new growth and life to a congregation. Many have done so in recent decades. There is usually some tension and conflict as some church members find that the new location will be too far from their home to be easily accessible, although any new location arrived at by democratic process is almost always within driving distance for the vast majority. But if church growth results from a move, it is because of more than a new address and facility. Location and equipment have something to do with which church people come to, but they are far down on the list for most people. If the "same old program" is what new people find in the new packaging, they will soon lose interest.

Although an initial influx of new members can be expected in any such move, no net gains in active membership will be realized unless issues beyond a new building are addressed. The positive outcomes in this option include the fact that it is easier to raise funds for a new physical plant than for the renovation of an old one, and the fact that the conventional pattern for success among Adventist churches has been to move to a new building. The primary negative is what is left undone—a decision about the target audience, ministry, and outreach strategy of the congregation. This option is primarily an institutional, and not a missional, alternative and cannot achieve growth by itself.

The Evangelism Center Alternative

In the postwar decade many denominational leaders developed the concept of establishing "permanent evangelistic centers" in the major cities. This strategy might still be viable. Most recently it has been proposed in the form of a church-based media ministry. Staffing must be much greater than the usual levels (associate

pastors, Bible workers, literature evangelists, etc.), and the conference must supplement the local budget, possibly the union conference as well. The pastor essentially ignores the existing congregation, leaving their care to an associate, and uses his time in planning
and conducting public evangelism. A regular schedule of Bible
classes is set up, and an advertising program established. This is
essentially an institutional and not a relational approach to evangelism.

The real question upon which the success of this strategy hangs
is this: Can the pastor get the necessary additional financial and
volunteer support from the congregation while at the same time
providing them with little or no programming or pastoral care?
Unless it can be realistically expected to baptize 100 to 200 persons
per year, the high cost of this option and the additional staff are not
justifiable in most local conferences. There is a real question as to
the probability of such results in many situations. The positive
factors in this option include the evangelistic results and the
potential impact on a large city.

The Church Planting Alternative

At times the best way to find new growth is to concentrate on
starting again with a new congregation. The established congregation becomes the "mother church," and those members interested
in a new style of worship and ministry "swarm" to form the core
of a new congregation. The mother church "grows" by sponsoring
the new "daughter" church. Conflict is avoided with church
members who are set in their ways and comfortable with things as
they are, and opportunity is afforded for those who want change to
make it happen in the new congregation. In the next chapter I
discuss this alternative in more detail.

A local conference might organize a pastoral team in a metropolitan area, with responsibility for consulting with small churches
already in existence and planting new churches. In cities of 1
million population or greater such an approach might reasonably be
expected to triple the number of Adventist congregations in a

decade. In view of the experience of other denominations, a six-year strategy to plant eight new congregations is entirely realistic. As the new congregations are planted, the character of the original congregations will change because members will transfer to new churches in their home communities. If strong programs are developed in the original churches, they would not cease to exist, although they may lose some membership. Total Adventist membership throughout the metropolitan area could reasonably be expected to grow at a rate of 5 percent a year or better once such a strategy reaches maturity.

The positive elements in this option include the favorable growth rate, the relatively "painless" method of introducing increased lay involvement in ministry, the small degree of social engineering required to create closer fellowship, the natural adaptation to appropriate forms for the various cultures involved both in nurture and outreach, and the relatively low cost. The negative elements here are the sophistication and newness of the concepts involved, the sense of "lost ground" that some members may feel as the emphasis moves away from big churches to small churches, and the difficulty of making a team ministry work.

Does Planning Make a Difference?

If congregations enter into a planning process, establish goals and strategies, does it really make any difference in their growth? Evidence that it does make a difference can be seen in the Boston Urban Ministries Project, which was supported by the NAD, the Atlantic Union Conference, and the Northeastern and Southern New England conferences from 1971 to 1977. This project represents a unique attempt to deal with the problems of city churches in one of the largest urban areas of the United States. Its purpose was "not simply evangelism or social service, but to be a catalyst for unleashing the proven evangelistic power of the laity in city churches." The project staff worked with local churches as consultants, helping them to conduct needs assessments, move through a planning process, and start small group ministries. "We have defined our ministry not as just another of many church programs to be added to the spectrum of things that the church is trying to accomplish," said a statement of purpose, "but as a specific, narrow tool to build up the total Seventh-day Adventist work in the city of Boston. Instead of seeking to bring in some new approach to replace, or to work alongside, the old approaches, we have sought to deal with the fundamental problems in the urban situation that seem to make failures of all approaches, new or old."[3]

Four specific methods were used in this church growth project. First, it was assumed that the local congregation was the church in mission and not just a constituency to support missionary projects that operate outside of it, and therefore outreach ministries were based in local congregations. Second, growth experiences were provided for the membership of the participating local churches, which stimulated, equipped, and enabled them to become more active in spontaneous witnessing among unchurched people. Third, educational programs were provided for local church pastors and lay leaders in which they learned to facilitate church growth as servant-leaders rather than simply pursue individual soulwinning. Fourth, consulting services and other resources were provided to local churches and mission groups on request. These four methods were designed to move the local church into closer contact with its ministry area and to mobilize the laity in ministry to that community, with the objective of rapidly increasing church growth.

What were the results of the project? There are at least three ways to answer this question. It could be answered in terms of soulwinning and church growth, or in terms of the attitudinal response of church members, or in terms of the impact made on the city. All three kinds of data will be presented here.

Perhaps the best way to get a view of the evangelistic impact of the project is to look at the overall growth rate of the churches involved. Figure 7 shows the total membership of all Adventist congregations in the Greater Boston area during the decade in question. The years of the project are marked off so that a comparison can be made. The rate of growth for Boston churches during

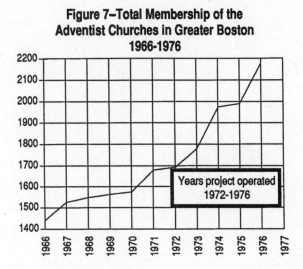

Figure 7–Total Membership of the
Adventist Churches in Greater Boston
1966-1976

Years project operated
1972-1976

the four years just prior to the project was 12 percent. During the four years of the project it was 23 percent. This means that the project helped to double the rate at which Boston churches were growing.

Figure 8 makes a more specific comparison between four local churches that elected not to participate in the planning/consulting process and five churches that participated fully. The participating churches had a growth rate about double that of the nonparticipating churches. The Boston project certainly demonstrates that consultants can work with churches to help them generate increased rates of growth.

To get a more specific evaluation of the Boston project, 55 church members were interviewed near the end of the project in 1977. Of these, 29 had been involved in the project, and the other 26 had never been involved in any way, but were congregational leaders interviewed for purposes of comparison. Of the 55 people interviewed, 64 percent were White, 31 percent were Black, and 5

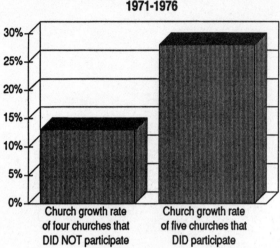

Figure 8–Comparative Rates of Church Growth 1971-1976

percent were from other racial backgrounds; 52 percent were members of suburban churches, and 48 percent were members of urban churches.

While a greater number of the noninvolved members indicated that "there are persons who because of my work and prayers have joined the Adventist Church as baptized members" (46 percent as compared to 34 percent), almost twice as many of the involved members indicated that they had interested persons either presently attending church or preparing for baptism at the time of the interview (38 percent as compared to 23 percent). When asked about their activity in evangelistic outreach, 41 percent of the project participants indicated they were active, while only 31 percent of the other church members were. Involvement in Adventist community service activities showed an even greater difference—24 percent of the project participants said they were involved in community service, while only 4 percent of the other church members said they were involved in community service. Almost equal numbers of project participants and nonparticipants indicated they held a church office (55 percent and 50 percent).

In rating their own spirituality, the nonparticipating church members were more likely to call themselves "strong" church members, but the participants were more likely to call themselves "active" church members. Almost three times as many of the nonparticipating members were willing to label themselves as "average" or "lukewarm" church members. Of those involved in the project, 79 percent said that it had helped to strengthen their spiritual lives; 72 percent said it had helped to make them more active in witnessing; 69 percent said it had helped to make them more effective in their witness; 55 percent felt that it had helped to make them more spontaneous in witnessing. Only 14 percent of the project participants answered these questions negatively.

About two thirds of those who participated felt that the Boston project had measurably assisted the growth of their local church. When given a list of specific activities of the project and asked to indicate which were most meaningful to the church in its missionary program, 55 percent selected the "model" entry events; 41 percent selected the workshops, retreats, and training events; and 34 percent selected the support groups. When asked about programs of the denomination outside the project that could, in their opinion, be strengthened or improved, 52 percent of the project participants said "lay training programs" and "the fellowship of believers," while only 25 percent of the other church members expressed the same concerns.

The project appears to have involved increasing numbers of church members as it continued; 17 percent of the participants indicated that they had been involved for four years or longer, while 45 percent said they had become involved in the past two or three years, and 14 percent said they had been involved for less than a year. The project also appears to have involved a much larger share of recent converts than church members of longer tenure. More than 48 percent of the project participants said they had been baptized for less than 20 years, while only 23 percent of the other church members were in this category. It seems that the project also did a good job of involving Adventists from religious backgrounds other than those from which the Adventist Church usually wins converts. Those who were Catholics, Baptists, or members of fundamentalist churches before they became Adventists included only 23 percent of the participants, but accounted for 46 percent of the other church members. More than 36 percent of the participants had come from liberal Protestant or unchurched backgrounds, while only 20 percent of the other church members shared this background.

From these data it is clear that those laymen and pastors who participated in the Boston project felt that it was successful in bringing growth and renewal to their churches. But what about the impact on the city outside the church? During the five years of the project, community services were provided to at least 40,000 individuals. Even if the success of the project were to be measured only by how much community outreach it generated, there is ample evidence that it did quite well.

Whether one looks at the project in terms of its impact on the larger community, or its impact on the renewal of churches, or its results in creating accessions to church membership, it was successful. The Boston project certainly demonstrates that churches can be helped to achieve greater growth and health through the intervention of a consulting process. Strategic planning can lead to greater evangelistic results.

---

1. Dick Jewett, in *Review and Herald*, Mar. 9, 1978, p. 3.

2. This entire process is described in greater detail and reproducible worksheets are supplied in Roger L. Dudley, ed., *A Manual for Church Growth Consulting* (Berrien Springs, Mich.: Institute of Church Ministry, 1987), chap. 4.

3. *Final Report of the Boston Urban Ministries Project*, p. 1.

CHAPTER 12
A Strategy for Metropolitan Areas

THE LARGE metropolitan areas of North America with their millions of unchurched young families must be reached with the gospel, and certain ingredients will be necessary to the strategy. The strategy will have to be developed city by city. The focus of the strategy will be the local church, although conferences have a special role to play to convene and support area-wide planning and vision.

What kind of support mechanisms can the denomination use to encourage local churches to attain growth and participate in a citywide strategy most effectively? Six key elements are discussed here because, among all the current suggestions, they appear to be the most effective means at hand.

The Urgent Need to Plant New Churches

Congregations, like human beings, have life cycles. Thousands of case histories of Protestant congregations have been carefully examined at the American Institute of Church Growth, and a pattern has emerged. After a congregation has existed for about 40 to 50 years, it enters into decline. In 9 out of 10 cases the congregation never pulls out of this dive, and within another 40 to 50 years it is dead.

I have looked at the full life cycle church growth data on hundreds of Adventist congregations in North America. Their pattern is the same, and I can add some specifics. Most Adventist congregations hit a plateau in their growth as soon as they purchase or build their own building. Very, very few become significantly larger in average Sabbath attendance than they are on the day the building is dedicated.

This means that if the denomination does not regularly add to its supply of congregations, eventually the sisterhood of churches across North America will be made up predominantly of static and declining bodies. We are dangerously close to that situation today. To document that for yourself, you need only look at your union paper and note the number of congregations celebrating anniversaries and centennials as compared to the number of new congregations being started.

A careful analysis of 375 new churches organized in the North American Division during the years 1977-1984 has been completed by Drs. Roger Dudley and Clarence Gruesbeck. They point out that "another reason for the Seventh-day Adventist Church in North America to plant more new churches relates to the observation by church leaders that Adventists tend to reach a very small segment of society." We need to reach a broader segment of society. In the 100 largest metropolitan areas in the U.S. and Canada, the majority of zip or postal code areas have no Adventist church and many lifestyle clusters have no active Adventist ministry designed to touch its particular needs.

Carefully planned and implemented, new congregations can broaden the outreach of the denomination so that it reaches people it would not otherwise touch. In general, existing churches fail to attract the unchurched. New congregations are less bound by inflexible traditions. The members of new congregations are more receptive to new ideas, new types of worship, and new ministries that appeal to more people.

Far from compromising church standards or beliefs, the new church provides a new approach for articulating solid Christian principles and more flexibility in ways evangelism can take place.

New congregations tend to be willing to accept people the way they are, while older congregations ask, "Why can't they be like us?"

That is why researcher Lyle Schaller reports, "Numerous studies have shown that 60 to 80 percent of new adult members of new congregations are persons who were not actively involved in the life of any church immediately prior to joining that new mission. . . . New Christians, as well as young adults born since 1940, are found in disproportionately larger numbers in new missions than in the older churches."

Some of these new adult members were youth who dropped out of the church in their teens or early 20s. Later, as parents, they want their children to have some religious training. They want to become involved in the church again. Preferring not to attend their parents' church, these young adults look for new types of worship.

Other former church attenders do not want to come back to the church where they severed relationships because they are embarrassed to return or fear that other members will not accept them. On the other hand, such people find acceptance in a new congregation where believers are used to welcoming new members.

There is abundant authority in the Bible for planting new congregations. This is particularly true in the book of Acts. It equates the multiplying of new Christian converts with the adding of new congregations (see Acts 16:5; 9:31). It teaches that Christianity is a religion based on relationships, and that new believers must be gathered into fellowship (Acts 2:41-47). Therefore, fellowship structures must be added to keep pace with the number of new converts.

Ellen White's vision for the Adventist Church also stresses the need for planting new churches. "Those who are the chosen of God are required to multiply churches wherever they may be successful in bringing souls to the knowledge of the truth," she writes. "New churches must be established, new congregations organized."[1] Throughout the history of the Adventist Church, the planting of new congregations has played a key role in its continued growth. In his research for the Doctor of Ministry degree, Larry Evans charted the growth or decline of membership in the Adventist Church against the organization of new congregations in the North American Division from 1910 to 1979. This study shows a positive correlation between membership growth and the number of new congregations organized.

The Texas Conference is an example of how planting new churches creates significant growth in membership in a conference. Over a period of eight years, 76 churches were established as a result of a church planting goal throughout the conference. During this time the number of converts more than doubled. During the six years prior to the church planting project, the most baptisms in any one year was 700. During the project, 1,900 were baptized in a single year.

With very few exceptions the rate at which a church can win people to faith in Christ, baptize them, and incorporate them into its fellowship will significantly increase when that church begins to meet in more than one place, or have more than one worship service each Sabbath.

Dudley and Gruesbeck have identified the essential ingredients for successfully starting a brand-new Seventh-day Adventist church. Their book *Plant a Church, Reap a Harvest* describes seven key elements in those new churches that had the best growth rates:

1. They were located in a large metropolitan area. The best place to plant a new church is in a city with a population of at least 50,000 or the suburbs of a large city. This is where the largest number of potential members are located.

2. They were sponsored by a "mother church" located within 3 to 10 miles. Proximity promotes growth and "competition" was not a problem for either the new church or the mother church. The more choices people have, the more of them join the church.

3. The mother church had 100 to 200 members. That may seem like too small a church to risk starting a new one, but even these relatively small congregations are not hurt by sponsoring a project to start a new church nearby.

4. The church planting project included a balanced program of evangelism. The efforts to start the new church included a mix of personal Bible studies, small group ministries, mailing of missionary magazines, a sequence of seminars that included health and family life topics, and public evangelism. Successful church planting projects have a "strategy" for initiating work among a new people group or in an unreached neighborhood.

5. A demographic study of the community was completed. The careful planning for the project began in most cases with fact-finding about the people living in the target area. And this information was used to "target" the activities of the church planting project and the new congregation.

6. The founding pastor had a democratic leadership style. Pastors who are successful in planting new churches are able to get church members involved in planning and decision-making, and in the implementation of the decisions.

7. They rented a place of worship for three to five years after being organized. The successful church planting projects do not rush into the purchase or construction of a new church building, but wait until the new congregation is mature enough to support a building program.

In 1989 the North American Division committee at its year-end meeting adopted a revised strategy document. It includes a priority goal of planting many new churches across the United States and Canada. This is a mandate for hundreds of church boards and mission groups to begin planning for new congregations which offer new styles of worship and ministry and reach out to new kinds of people.

New congregations are the lifeline of the denomination. Unless a new generation of recently formed churches is constantly brought on line, we run the risk of stagnation and decline. Every metropolitan area has many neighborhoods and suburban towns where there is presently no Adventist church. Over the decade of the 1990s, 1,000 to 2,000 new Adventist congregations could be started in North America.

Encouraging Small Group Ministries

It does not matter if they are called "Homes of Hope," house churches, cottage meetings, mission groups, or Home Bible Fellowships; small groups are essential to the evangelization of the metropolitan areas of North America. This is true because of both internal and external factors influencing metro area congregations. The typical Adventist congregation has what church growth experts call a "single cell" fellowship. That is to say that there is essentially one grouping of people involved in lay activities and fellowship in a congregation. In small town and rural churches, this presents no difficulty, because the community which the church is trying to win often has a single culture. As new people come into the church they find it relatively easy to feel right at home. In city and suburban churches there is much variety in the kinds of people because the metropolitan environment is multicultural. A number of different fellowship "cells" are needed within a city church just to hold the existing members. In turn, a variety of different lay ministries are required in order to reach the vast mosaic of people groups in the metropolis.

Adventist churches in the great urban centers must become what are sometimes called "base churches"—congregations that become a base of operations for a wide range of small groups and lay ministries. A "base church" is a church that constantly feeds and supports outreach projects, and welcomes and cares for the new converts as they are brought in. It is a church that thrives on a variety of people, making room for each new kind of lifestyle and for each set of needs. It is a congregation honeycombed with many different kinds of fellowship cells and activity groups. Ellen White envisioned this concept, and in one of her most detailed descriptions of what she saw as the model of a successful, growing city church, she called it a "beehive" of activity.[2]

The business of turning declining churches into strong, active churches is difficult and problematic. Few Adventist pastors have been trained in the concepts and techniques of church renewal, and often there is not strong support from conference administrators for the changes that need to be made in order to bring about renewal. Perhaps a feasible way to begin church renewal in a metropolitan area is for one particular congregation to be sought as a "volunteer" to become the base church for new ministries, and to concentrate on renewing and building up that congregation, leaving the others to become "havens" for those church members who are not comfortable with the emphasis on small groups. This base church could become the sponsor for church-planting projects, and over a period of a decade or two the entire picture of church life in that metropolitan area might be changed with a minimum of conflict.

The evangelistic activity of the Adventist Church is at present heavily invested in public meetings and media ministries. The need to develop a strategy of small group evangelism ought not to be seen as a replacement for the existing efforts. In fact, to "wipe the slate clean" and begin again to build a new strategy would result in enormous dislocation and loss. Rather, it is important to find ways to integrate a new emphasis on small groups with the conventional approach so that they interact with each other in a supportive way. Media programs and public meetings can be fine-tuned to enhance and benefit from the newly emerging small group ministries.

Reshaping Media Outreach

Soul-winning success through the involvement of church members in small group ministries can be facilitated with the strategic use of the mass media. Random, unrelated witnessing activities can easily be lost in the massive scale of a large metropolitan area. On the other hand, marketing tools available today can enable personal communication with mass audiences. An illustration of the possibilities can be seen in the way a psychologist with a radio talk show becomes the trusted advisor of tens of thousands of people, or a grandmother in a television commercial for hamburgers becomes a household name.

The Adventist Church is not presently near the potential of media ministry in the cities. The primary lack is in strategy, not products. When a major advertising campaign is launched to sell soap, 10 to 50 times as much airtime is used as in Adventist broadcast evangelism. This airtime is purchased with very sophisticated targeting to specific audiences, using the array of demographic data that is available. A properly targeted media campaign is essential to evangelistic success in the large cities not only because it will bring people into meetings and programs, but also because it lends credibility to the overall institutional image, or "positioning," of the church.

Saturation use of radio and television to build public awareness in a city will include both spot announcements and longer programs on a regular year-round basis. It will include locally produced elements as well as national broadcasts. In every major metropolitan area, all of the nationwide Adventist radio and television ministries should be on the air, each targeted to the unique people group that it reaches. The local programs should be targeted toward the kinds of people that are not being reached by the national programs.

For example, a weekly 30-minute television program could be produced, featuring a local pastor and a physician as the hosts. The topics could be tied to themes suggested in the health ministries of the local churches. Three to five minutes of documentary film could be used to grab viewer attention at the beginning of each show. The rest of the program might be an informal dialogue with a small studio audience. This kind of program could regularly publicize the seminars and small group activities of local churches, and names of interested persons could be gathered by offers of free information. Included might be the advertising of regular Bible study classes throughout the metropolitan area. This kind of programming could be produced with local talent available in many cities, and might be accepted as a public service (at no cost) on some stations or sponsored by an Adventist Health System institution. Both radio and television broadcasts of this type have been tried successfully in New York and Vancouver.

The potential of spot programming (30-second or 60-second messages) has been ignored by Adventist media ministries until recently. In the large cities more money would be well invested in awareness-building spots than in longer programs. It is the peculiar nature of fast-paced urban and suburban life that the majority of the people can never be reached by religious programming of 5, 15, or 30 minutes' duration. Less than 3 percent of the American population is being reached by traditional religious broadcasts, and one of the major reasons is simply program length.[3] Spot programming can be targeted toward specific audiences with greater precision than longer programming, although the need for sophisticated planning is also greater than with conventional forms of media ministry.

A principle of mass communication that needs to be more fully understood and used more widely by the church is tied up in the difference between what is called "institutional" advertising and "product" advertising. As applied to media evangelism, this concept means that spot ads need to be used to "sell" an awareness of the Adventist Church, as well as to present information about a specific series of meetings or a particular service or piece of literature available to the public. The advertising industry has come to realize that the best sales results come from using both kinds at the same time. A good example of this can be seen in the advertising strategy of the McDonald's Corporation. Some television spots sell McDonald's restaurants as nice, friendly places that care about people. Other spots sell the food items themselves. Adventist evangelization needs the same kind of mixed media strategy tied to its caring churches and the specific services offered by its members.

This approach was tested in 1989 in Spokane, Washington, by the NAD United Marketing Taskforce, a group of Adventist media and church ministries specialists. In before and after surveys using random telephone interviews, 62 percent of the residents were found to have seen the spots. And 75 percent of these folk knew that the Adventist Church was the "product" and said that they liked the commercials. One in five said that they would be more likely to attend church after viewing the spots, and 12 percent said they would be more likely to join the Adventist Church. "That translates into something in the neighborhood of 30,000 to 40,000 people in Spokane who are more likely to join the Seventh-day Adventist Church now than before the commercials aired," says Dr. Kermit Netteburg, a project consultant. Baby boomers were more likely to see the spots and respond positively than were those older than 45. The project has successfully identified and tested a marketing position that will market the Adventist Church in large metropolitan areas: The Seventh-day Adventist Church is the family that is there when you need us.

"We've had considerable discussion about whether the church truly is the family that is there when people need help," comments Netteburg. "We've come to two conclusions. First, if the church is not there when it is needed, the church probably has little rationale to exist. Second, the Seventh-day Adventist Church is probably more frequently ready to help nonmembers than members, and our marketing position is a position targeted to nonmembers." Of course, if members feel that their needs are not met, they will tell potential members, and that will destroy church growth. And the local churches described in this volume have demonstrated that the church can meet needs in an effective way.

An effective media strategy will also be long-term. The real payoff from advertising does not come in a few weeks, but after the residual buildup of years of continuous usage, with regular updating of presentations, but one or two constant images that are etched into the subconscious of the mass audience. One place where that has begun to occur for the Adventist Church is New York City, where such a strategy has been used by the van ministry for nearly a decade, and a real impact on the church growth rate can now be measured.

Print media also need to be a part of a total media outreach in the metropolitan areas. Consistent and well-designed direct-mail advertising is perhaps the least expensive way to contact new people for the first time and to bring initial contacts to entry events and on into pathways to church membership. Direct mail could also be used to build the audience for broadcast ministries, to sell Adventist books, and to enroll people in Bible correspondence courses. For example, a quarterly newspaper insert could be circulated to target zip codes or blocks within a metropolitan area. Mail-order sale of paperback missionary books, and advertising from the Publishing Department, Adventist Book Centers, and other institutions might help pay for the publication. Each issue might advertise the most current public seminars being presented in the metropolitan area. Included could be stories about individuals helped by community service ministries, as well as presentations of the worship, Bible study, small groups, Christian education, and youth activities of the churches.

Public Meetings

Public meetings continue to be a key element in reaching the metropolitan areas. A strategy of public meetings that takes into consideration what the data demonstrate concerning the importance of involving church members in community service and properly assimilating new converts will not only function as a "reaping" mechanism but also serve to contact many people for the first time. Such a strategy is not at odds with an emphasis on small groups. In fact, a regular cycle of large group meetings is supported by and supportive of a strong program of small groups. They can function in a dynamic way, feeding each other while caring for the audiences that both serve separately. Seminars are an appropriate format for public meetings today because they utilize a style widely known to unchurched people from business and schooling, and because they partake of some of the elements of small group dynamics. The most effective public seminars have an attendance of 25 to 50.[4]

Experimentation by Mark Finley and others demonstrates that if this strategy includes a balanced schedule of health, mental health, and religious topics, there are enhanced results, reaching a wide variety of people. Previous and current failures with "health evangelism" stem largely from a strategy that leaps from physical needs all the way to spiritual needs—a distance too great for people to follow. The sequencing of needs allows for a natural progression from physical needs to emotional needs to spiritual needs. A "bridging" step has been supplied with the stress clinic and related types of family life seminars, and there are many other possibilities to be explored.

Successful use of public meetings in metropolitan areas will include a regular yearly cycle in each local church. During the first quarter of each cycle (not necessarily the first quarter of the calendar year), a health screening and education series will be presented: a health fair or "Heartbeat" program, nutrition class, Breathe-Free Plan, etc. During the second quarter of each cycle, a seminar in the "bridge" or mental health category will be presented: stress management, family life, grief recovery, etc. During the third quarter of the cycle a preevangelism seminar will be presented, such as the Daniel Seminar. During the last quarter a Revelation Seminar or other full-message series will be presented.

The cycle will begin again in the first quarter of the new program year. Entry to the people flow in this cycle will occur at each stage, as those are reached who are at that point in their felt needs. Some people will come for the first time during the doctrinal meetings, and for them the rest of the cycle will serve as a process of nurture to strengthen them in the Adventist lifestyle. Others of a more secular orientation will come for the first time during the phases where the emphasis is on physical or emotional needs, and be introduced to spiritual concepts. Of course, there will be dropouts all along the way, but the total effect will be a more consistent accession pattern and a greater rate of real growth in discipling.

Smaller churches will implement this strategy on a smaller scale than larger churches, but it has been demonstrated that no church is too small to carry on this kind of annual public program within the constraints of current funding policies of the North American Division. Larger churches may implement more than one cycle a year. Two or more cycles could be run simultaneously in two or more sections of the community. It is essential that in each case an equal amount of public advertising be given to each phase of the cycle and that key sessions of the seminars in each phase be conducted outside the church building.

Metro Ministry Coordinator

The Adventist Church can never mount a serious effort to reach the large metropolitan areas until it develops church growth specialists and invests in adequate staffing for each of the major cities. This is essential because so few pastors have specialized training in urban ministry. The building of an effective metropolitan strategy is a long-term task, but pastors tend to stay in city churches for relatively short periods and there is high turnover among church members, too. Therefore the continuity of a central coordinating office is vital in each metropolitan area. Effectively reaching the cities is also a very complex task, calling for the cooperation of all of the local churches in a metropolitan area and for the planting of new churches. Because of the organizational loyalty that is necessarily a trait of each local pastor and congregation, the total task will not be addressed unless there is a coordinator that stands outside any specific local congregation and speaks for the total mission of the church. A metro ministry coordinator can also provide the consultant skills necessary to enable a high level of goal ownership in local congregations.

Our city churches are, by and large, not prospering. Especially in the large metroplexes in the northeastern United States, non-ethnic Adventist congregations are not growing. A simple measurement of the health of these congregations, as suggested by C. Peter Wagner's model for church pathology, indicates why there is no growth.[5] A great number of the "White" churches in the large cities have a good case of what Wagner calls "St. John's Syndrome." That is, they are made up largely of third- and fourth-generation descendants of the founders and early converts of that local church. These people are usually middle-aged and older, and have little motivation or capacity to do more than survive. Added to this, in many cases, is a second condition that Wagner calls "people blindness." Often 80 percent of the congregation commutes from the suburbs to attend a city church and are completely out of touch with the local population in the neighborhood where the church building is located. They do not see the differences in culture, demographics, and needs that exist between the suburban communities where they live and the church's ministry area. Therefore when outreach projects are planned by the local church, these projects usually fail.[6]

In some congregations these conditions have continued for so many years that yet a third "disease" has set in to complicate the situation even further. These congregations have what Wagner calls "koinonitis." They have "inflamed fellowship patterns," with a very ingrown set of relationships that makes it difficult for new members to become assimilated into the congregation. This is especially true if these new members are converts from an unchurched background or a different lifestyle than that of the established members, but it is true even for Adventists transferring in from out of town.

During my ministry in Northeastern cities, I have had occasion to visit with a large number of Adventists who moved in from the South or West because of jobs or to get advanced education, and in many of these cases they dropped out of church participation and did not seek to transfer their membership, because they perceived themselves as not fitting into the congregation. When a congregation gets to this point of "ill health" many of its members become outspokenly resistant to any kind of evangelism. In my discussions with city pastors from other regions, I am told that this is not an isolated situation, but one that is present in many urban congregations.

All of this argues for the need of a real program of church renewal among urban congregations. Significant lay witnessing is not going to be a reality unless there is a change of attitude and priorities on the part of these congregations. In fact, no amount of increased effectiveness in the evangelization of metropolitan areas will result in church growth if there is not a renewal of congregations. When new converts are won, it is essential that there be receptive, nurturing churches for them to establish membership in. The necessary degree of church renewal will not become a reality with "business as usual" in the denomination. It needs special staffing resources.

For maximum effectiveness, a metro area coordinating team would include four people:

1. A director who has consultant skills and is capable of dealing with research, program development, and strategy.

2. A Bible worker who can serve as the interest coordinator for the entire metropolitan area and as a witnessing trainer for the local churches.

3. An associate director who has skills in the areas of health and community service ministry, as well as some training in marketing and media relations.

4. An experienced administrative secretary who is bilingual.

All of the available evidence from church growth research suggests that the Adventist mission to major metropolitan areas would gain much more from this kind of staffing pattern than from expanding the pastoral staffs of large city churches, especially in the suburbs. These pastoral staffers become focused professionally and functionally on maintenance. A metro ministry staff would be focused on mission. Would it be a "doable" goal to have such a team established in each metropolitan area of more than 1 million population by the end of this century?

Continued Research

It is essential that there be careful, consistent research in each major metropolitan area before a new thrust of evangelism and church growth begins there. The complex dynamics of urbanization are not well understood by a large number of Adventist workers, even many of those who are committed to metropolitan ministry. No strategy can be effective in reaching a city unless insight is first gained to its mosaic of people groups, cultural values, and social dynamics. This involves more than demographics. An adequate data base for a given metropolitan area would include:

1. Identifying the people groups and lifestyle clusters within the metropolitan area, and the character of each unit in terms of its values, socioeconomic structure, geographic location, etc.[7]

2. Surveying the Adventist membership to find out which people groups have been penetrated by Adventists, how the membership came to join the church, and other local patterns of church growth.[8]

3. Evaluating the Adventist churches as to their health, growth patterns, and readiness for a stronger mission emphasis.

4. Collecting available research on the religious patterns, church membership in all denominations, and general values of the population.[9]

5. Having conversations with key leaders in the various neighborhoods to determine what kinds of programs already exist so that Adventist community service outreaches are not seen as duplication.

6. Visiting each of the neighborhoods to observe the patterns, needs, and opportunities that will indicate the kinds of approaches which will work best in that community.

This information will not be of any use unless it is also displayed in graphics that pastors and lay leaders can quickly understand and use. These graphics should be designed not only to present facts, but to call forth the commitment of the people to the great task of reaching the metropolis.

Amateur attempts in this area of research will not lend strength to these efforts. Dr. Gottfried Oosterwal, director of the Institute of World Mission, has proposed the establishment of urban institutes to carry on this work. The proper staff working from such an institute could prepare high-quality research and interpret it in a professional manner. This kind of consulting service could serve to initiate effective strategies for metropolitan ministry in many areas. The staff of the institute could also monitor experimental efforts throughout the field and communicate to church leaders what is working and what is not working. Such an institute would not need to be very expensive because it does not require full-time staffing. A metropolitan institute could be operated by a small committee and arrange to borrow or pay for services from appropriate college and university faculty, pastors, denominational staffers, and qualified professionals among the laity as needed for various projects and studies. The institute might also sponsor a training school for pastors, evangelists, and lay leaders to be attended by a select group for about 10 days each year.

Conclusion

Among the actions of the 1980 General Conference session was a call for special attention to reaching the secular and non-Christian peoples of the world, and the large cities. At the 1985 General Conference session the president, Elder Neal C. Wilson, reaffirmed "the challenge of the cities" as a major priority of the denomination and quoted Ellen White's comments from the 1909 session: "O, that we might see the needs of these great cities as God sees them." "It is distressing that they have been neglected so long."[10]

At the same time, it seems that there is little activity by Adventists for the evangelization of the major metropolitan areas of North America. The denomination seems to be engaged in a massive withdrawal from the cities. There is less funding for evangelism and church growth. The moving of churches to the fringes continues, a trend now joined by Black and Hispanic congregations. Very few pastors actually live in the neighborhoods where their churches are located, and there is a continued reduction of pastoral staffing for the metropolitan areas. If the Adventist Church does not begin to reach the large cities, it will not only lose a major opportunity for evangelization, but it will also suggest that it is not serious about the task of reaching every nation, kindred, tongue, and people with the three angels' messages.

———————

1. Ellen G. White, *Testimonies to Ministers* (Mountain View, Calif.: Pacific Press Pub. Assn., 1923), p. 199; *Testimonies*, vol. 6, p. 24.

2. ———,*Welfare Ministry* (Washington, D.C.: Review and Herald Pub. Assn., 1952), p. 112.

3. James F. Engel cited this research during the church growth seminar at Andrews University, August 1-5, 1981. It was also reported in a publication distributed to denominational workers by Faith for Today in the spring of 1981.

4. Lyle Schaller, "The Rule of 40," *The Christian Ministry* (September 1983), pp. 11, 12.

5. C. Peter Wagner, *Your Church Can Be Healthy* (Nashville: Abingdon, 1979).

6. One of the 10 most important factors in Adventist church growth is a "thorough study of the local community" (see R. Dudley and D. Cummings, *Factors Relating to Church Growth,* pp. 64, 65).

7. The North American Division marketing program has been developed as a highly sophisticated tool for this purpose. Interdenominational experts believe it is the most sophisticated market analysis tool among all denominations in North America. Access to data for each local area is available through the Institute of Church Ministry at Andrews University.

8. The Institute of Church Ministry has developed three basic survey tools that can be used in collecting this information. These surveys are designed for church members, new members, and pastors.

9. Bernard Quinn et al., *Churches and Church Membership in the United States: 1980* (Atlanta: Glenmary Research Center, 1982).

10. *General Conference Bulletin* No. 1, *Adventist Review*, June 27, 1985, p. 8.